A$$ET
PROTECTION

HAROLD HUDSON

A$$ET
PROTECTION

Planning for **Business Owners, Real Estate Operators, Professionals,** and **Investors** in

GEORGIA

Published by Advantage, Charleston, South Carolina.
Member of Advantage Media Group.

ADVANTAGE is a registered trademark, and the Advantage colophon is a trademark of Advantage Media Group, Inc.

Printed in the United States of America.

10 9 8 7 6 5 4 3 2 1

ISBN: 978-1-59932-529-3
LCCN: 2017933416

Advantage Media Group is proud to be a part of the Tree Neutral® program. Tree Neutral offsets the number of trees consumed in the production and printing of this book by taking proactive steps such as planting trees in direct proportion to the number of trees used to print books. To learn more about Tree Neutral, please visit **www.treeneutral.com.**

Advantage Media Group is a publisher of business, self-improvement, and professional development books. We help entrepreneurs, business leaders, and professionals share their Stories, Passion, and Knowledge to help others Learn & Grow. Do you have a manuscript or book idea that you would like us to consider for publishing? Please visit **advantagefamily.com** or call **1.866.775.1696.**

TABLE OF CONTENTS

WARNING AND DISCLAIMER

This book provides general information to Georgia businesses and residents about how to structure their affairs to help protect their assets from lawsuits and attorneys who want to take those assets. This book is not intended as a substitute for a practitioner's own research, or for the advice of a qualified tax adviser or a qualified attorney. Each person who reads this book must come to his or her own conclusions as to the proper course of action to take. The author and publisher shall have neither liability nor responsibility to any person or entity with respect to any loss or damage caused, or alleged to be caused, directly or indirectly, by the information contained in this book.

This book is *not* intended to give you legal or tax advice about *your specific* situation, for that can only be done by an attorney who you engage or hire and who understands your unique circumstances. When I am not writing books, I am a practicing attorney (since 1988). As much as my clients and I wish, there is no such thing as a "one-size-fits-all" legal solution or form document to fix different people's different circumstances. Accordingly, you need to engage an attorney, so he or she can create a solution for your unique situation.

To become a client of mine or my firm, you and I must sign a written engagement letter setting forth the specific terms of the work that my firm or I will perform for you, including but not limited to the fee to perform the work. You are not my client if you and I do not sign an engagement letter.

C H A P T E R 1

PROTECTING YOUR VALUABLE ASSETS

This book explains how Georgia business owners, real estate operators, professionals, and investors can protect their valuable assets. More specifically, the book is written for Georgia residents who (a) own and operate businesses, (b) own and operate residential and commercial real estate, (c) have accumulated wealth, or (d) are professionals such as attorneys, dentists, doctors, engineers, architects, or accountants.

This book examines and explains Georgia laws concerning (a) trusts, (b) debtor and creditor rights, (c) partnerships, (d) limited liability companies, (e) corporations, (f) contract provisions to limit liability, (g) liability of professionals to patients and clients, (h) using arbitration clauses to avoid court battles, (i) when a gift or transfer of assets is a "fraudulent transfer" that can be voided by a creditor, and (j) other legal strategies and concepts relating to protection of valuable assets.

Georgia laws relevant to asset-protection planning are different, and in some cases very different, from the laws of other states, even neighboring states. For example:

- Florida and Texas limit the amount a patient can recover in a medical malpractice lawsuit. Georgia previously had a limit on noneconomic damages (sometimes called "pain and suffering") in medical malpractice lawsuits, but the Georgia Supreme Court recently ruled that the law was unconstitutional, so Georgia no longer caps noneconomic damages.

- Tennessee, Mississippi, and fourteen other states allow a resident to establish a trust for his or her own benefit, transfer assets to the trust, and exempt the trust assets from certain creditors of the resident. Georgia expressly prohibits these types of trusts, commonly referred to as "self-settled trusts."

- Florida permits a resident who files bankruptcy to shelter the cash value of a life insurance policy—regardless of value—from creditors. Georgia law only protects $2,000 of the cash value of the life insurance policy from bankruptcy creditors.

- Florida permits a resident who files bankruptcy to shelter the entire value of his principal residence/homestead from certain creditors. Georgia law only protects up to $21,500 of the value of a Georgia resident's principal residence.

- When a landlord files a lawsuit against a tenant for rent, Georgia law only permits the landlord to be reimbursed for attorney fees in an amount equal to 15 percent of the unpaid rent. In most situations, the actual attorney fees paid by the landlord exceed 15 percent of the unpaid rent. Florida does not cap reimbursement of attorney fees by landlords, and only requires the fees to be "reasonable."

Throughout the book, actual cases decided by Georgia courts are used to illustrate concepts and strategies. The reason for using actual cases is to show the reader that the concepts and issues presented in the book are very real and greatly affect people's lives. Georgia cases are used to show you—the Georgia resident—how you will likely be treated if you find yourself in a lawsuit in Bibb County (Macon), Fulton County (Atlanta), Hall County (Gainesville), Glynn County (Brunswick, Sea Island, St. Simons), Whitfield County (Dalton), or any of the other 154 counties in Georgia.

From time to time, people will tell me that they have read an article about the benefits of forming a corporation, trust, or LLC in a state other than Georgia (e.g., Nevada or Delaware), and they ask me whether doing so in another state is advisable. There is a lot of confusion (and misleading information on the Internet) about forming entities in Nevada, Delaware, and other states, and this topic is addressed fully in chapter 7. However, it should be made clear that if you live in Georgia and you have dealings with other Georgia residents and businesses, you will have to examine and deal with the laws of the state of Georgia.[1] For example, Georgia law—not the law of any other state—determines: (a) important rights between Georgia landlords and residential tenants; (b) the validity of restrictive covenants on employees working in Georgia; (c) the validity of a prenuptial agreement made in Georgia between Georgia residents;

---

1   Under Georgia Code Section 1-3-9, parties to a contract can agree to apply the law of another state to the contract, but even if the contract provides for that, Georgia law, not the law of the other state, will apply if the law of the chosen state is contrary to Georgia public policy.

and (d) your liability when you drive your car negligently and injure another person in Georgia.

CHAPTER 1 RECAP:

The laws that relate to protecting your assets vary greatly from state to state, and Georgia residents must understand Georgia laws and engage Georgia lawyers.

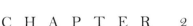

WHAT IS THE GEORGIA COMPREHENSIVE ASSET PROTECTION PLANNING™ PROCESS?

"Planning" is defined in the dictionary as the process of preparing for a future event.

To be ready for a catastrophic storm like a hurricane requires planning before the rotating storm clouds appear on the radar. In hurricane-prone areas, homes must be specially designed and built by architects and builders to withstand violent winds and water; shelters must be designated; emergency provisions must be purchased and stored; evacuation routes must be studied with care; every few years, you must reevaluate your precautions and purchase new emergency provisions; and you must remain on guard and conscious of the weather. The hope, of course, is that the lives of the people who live in hurricane-prone areas and their valuable coastal homes and properties will not be destroyed by the direct hit of a hurricane, but

HAROLD HUDSON ▶ 5

if a hurricane *does* come, the homeowner will be as ready as possible. Will all the houses and condos situated along the Florida coasts suffer a hit by a hurricane? Probably not, but history shows us that many lives and properties can suddenly suffer a direct hit and be destroyed by a powerful hurricane.

For the people who live in hurricane-prone areas, planning for a hurricane requires extra precautions, but the extra precautions are not hardships that adversely affect the lives of those people. To the contrary, having taken the extra precautions, these people have less anxiety and know that their precious lives and valuable investments will be protected and allowed to flourish in the future. The people who are "hurricane ready" are far less likely to lose their investments and have to start over.

Like preparing for a hurricane, planning to protect your assets requires specific, detailed steps to be taken by you *before* someone tries to take your valuable assets from you. As we will see in chapter 3, the people who can take your assets include, but certainly are not limited to: an employee; a tenant of a house or building you own; a patient; a client; a customer who is injured at your business; a person who is injured by your employee; a business partner; and a spouse in a divorce. Like planning for a hurricane, planning to protect your assets requires extra precautions that are specifically designed to reduce or eliminate the threat—but the extra precautions themselves are not hardships. People who take specific steps to protect their assets have less anxiety and are less likely to have to start over and work to replace their lost assets with new ones.

Have you ever heard someone say "Rich people are lucky" or "A black cloud seems to follow him because he has such bad luck in business"? These expressions are nonsense. People who are financially successful are very deliberate and thoughtful. The "black cloud of bad luck" is made by people who are not prepared and who do not plan.

Unless you won the lottery, your wealth and valuable assets did not just materialize overnight. They were created by *planning steps*:

- You improved yourself through study, school, and/or work experience.

- You worked hard.

- You watched your expenses and denied yourself.

- You saved.

- You invested.

- You took calculated risks.

- You repeated the above steps over and over and over.

"Georgia Comprehensive Asset Protection Planning" is the process whereby Georgia residents (or businesses) systematically arrange and manage their affairs to minimize the likelihood of a lawsuit being filed against them—and if someone tries to file lawsuit—the appropriate legal structures and arrangements are in place to minimize the loss of assets.

Georgia Comprehensive Asset Protection Planning requires you to take the following eight steps:

1. Identify every asset and income that you have now.

2. Identify every asset and income that you may acquire in the future (for example, an inheritance from your parents).

3. Identify every potential source of liability you have now.

4. Identify every arrangement you have where either you pay someone to perform services for you or you perform services for someone else.

5. Review your liability insurance policies and coverage and, if necessary, make adjustments.

6. Implement contract and legal strategies to minimize or eliminate liability.

7. Implement legal strategies to safeguard your assets.

8. Repeat steps one through seven over and over because your assets, incomes, liabilities, business relationships, etc. change through the years.

With Georgia Comprehensive Asset Protection Planning, the details of your business and financial affairs are audited, strategies for your particular situation are identified, and those strategies are implemented.

For example, in many instances, the contracts you have with other persons or companies should provide that in the event of a dispute: (a) the dispute will be settled quickly by a professional arbitrator who is familiar with the subject of the contract, whom you know to be of high character and experience, and who is

> **DON'T EVEN TRY!** You can't hide your assets from anyone these days due to the following:
>
> - credit-reporting agencies
> - online real estate records
> - online access to county tax records
> - online access to business-formation and filing records from governmental agencies, such as the Corporation Division of the Georgia Secretary of State
> - private investigators
> - Internal Revenue Service reporting requirements
> - social media websites like Facebook and LinkedIn
> - online photographs of your home and other real estate on Google Earth

located near you; and (b) the loser will pay all the costs, including the arbitrator's fee and the winner's legal fees. In almost no circumstance do you want to be thrown into the court system, where the judge and the jury may not know or care about the subject matter *or you*, where your trial attorney makes money whether you win or lose, where your case could drag on for years before getting to trial, and where everyone in the world can read all the court claims (which may be false) and details of your personal and business affairs. Moreover, you want the person who files a lawsuit against you to bear your legal fees and costs—assuming you win. In Georgia, it is very rare for the loser of a lawsuit to be required to pay for the winner's legal fees (unless, perhaps, a contract requires the loser to pay).

Georgia Comprehensive Asset Protection Planning does not involve hiding or trying to hide your assets or activities. For twenty-five dollars, in about thirty minutes, a lawyer can find out 80 percent of what your financial life looks like. In several hours, and for a little more money, 95 percent of your financial life can be discovered. It seems that the quest for information on people grows daily. For example, under the Foreign Account Tax Compliance Act, which became effective on July 1, 2014, offshore financial institutions are required to automatically transfer information about their American clients to the Internal Revenue Service.

Most people with valuable assets have engaged in basic asset protection by purchasing liability insurance to cover harm they may cause to other people and their property. You buy liability insurance and malpractice insurance with the hope that the insurance will be sufficient to cover any harm you cause so that you do not have to use your own money and assets to pay for the damages. However, as we will see below, your insurance may not be sufficient to cover the damages, *or* your insurance policy may contain an "exclusion" that negates the coverage, *or* you may be sued for something for which you do not have insurance (such as a lawsuit by your partner or a claim for discrimination by an employee). Georgia Comprehensive Asset Protection Planning involves much more than purchasing liability insurance.

Asset-protection planning is not new. One of the first projects I worked on when I started practicing law in Florida in 1988 involved asset-protection planning for a doctor. Corporate and tax lawyers have been advising clients on how to protect their assets for many, many years.

Anyone who cares about his or her financial affairs—and family—should undertake Georgia Comprehensive Asset Protection Planning ... *now*. Procrastination can result in terrible problems—and they can happen to the best of us. Take, for example, people who have not made a last will and testament or who have not revised it for many years. There is a 100 percent certainty that we are all going to die, so everyone should have an updated will! Yet some people never make one or put off updating an old, outdated one. Why? Surely these unprepared people care about their families and want to provide for and protect their families for as long as possible after they

> Comprehensive asset-protection planning is not difficult; however, it requires a lawyer who understands the following types of law in Georgia:
>
> - income tax law
> - estate tax law
> - gift tax law
> - bankruptcy law
> - corporate law
> - creditor rights law
> - trust law
> - partnership law
> - contract law

are no longer able to. Surely they don't have matters more pressing or important than providing for their families. Surely they know that the cost of getting a Last Will and Testament is not expensive. In any case, don't procrastinate—begin Georgia Comprehensive Asset Protection Planning now. It is easy and not expensive.

CHAPTER 2 RECAP:

1. Planning and preparedness will produce good results; lack of planning and failure to prepare will result in the loss of assets.

2. The goals of Georgia Comprehensive Asset Protection Planning are to (1) minimize the chance that someone will file a lawsuit against you, (2) stay out of the court system if possible, and (3) minimize the monetary harm of a loss by having the correct legal structure in place.

3. An example of Georgia Comprehensive Asset Protection Planning is to add an arbitration clause to your contracts that requires a dispute or claim for damages to be settled quickly and privately by an arbitrator who is not part of the court system. The arbitrator will be a person who understands the subject of the contract. The arbitration clause will require the loser to pay the winner's attorney fees, a disincentive to frivolous lawsuits.

4. Georgia Comprehensive Asset Protection Planning is not difficult and it is not expensive, but you must take action! Congratulations—reading this book is a great first step!

C H A P T E R 3

START AUDITING YOURSELF: IDENTIFYING THE LEGAL RISKS OF YOUR ACTIVITIES

Recently, I heard a judge in Fulton County Court in Atlanta tell the jury the following before the trial began:

> *"Please pay careful attention. You have a very serious job. The lives and finances of the people involved in this case are in your hands. You or a relative or a friend could very easily be a party to a lawsuit, and if that were the case, you would want the jury to be attentive and do their best job."*

Can bad things happen to good people? Yes.

Do we all make mistakes? Yes.

Can you be sued? Yes.

In 2014, there were 770,710 civil (noncriminal) lawsuits filed in magistrate, state, and superior courts in Georgia![2] And that does not

---

2   *Annual Report FY 2015*, Judicial Council of Georgia, Administrative Office of the Courts.

include the 151,672 divorce cases.[3] The people who file these lawsuits (known as plaintiffs) are generally trying to get money from other people (the defendants). A plaintiff does not usually file a lawsuit unless he or she thinks the defendant has money and/or assets. Thus, if you or your business has money or assets, you or your business is a target for a lawsuit. As the judge warned, any of us can find ourselves as the defendant in a lawsuit.

Sometimes I come across people who do not realize or appreciate the "legal risk" of the activities in which they are engaged.

"Legal risk" involves the following analysis:

a) What is the chance that I will get sued for engaging in a particular activity?

b) How much money could I get sued for?

c) What is the probability that the person who sues me will be awarded a lot of money?

d) Will I have to use my money and assets to pay part or all of the court judgment against me?

I saw a good example of "legal risk" recently on Interstate 75 between Atlanta and Macon. An 8,500-pound truck owned by a construction company was being driven by an employee of the company. Let's call the driver Edward. There were three coworkers in the truck. The truck was speeding (it passed me like I was standing still) in heavy traffic on Friday afternoon, and Edward was sending text messages or e-mails on his cell phone. Edward's actions have a high legal risk for the construction company and Edward himself

---

3   Ibid.

because: (a) there is a good chance Edward will cause a wreck due to looking at his phone and away from the traffic-laden road; (b) the 8,500-pound SUV traveling in excess of seventy-five miles per hour may cause serious damage to other automobiles and can cause serious physical injury—even death—to the coworkers riding with Edward as well as occupants of other cars, so damages could be as high as millions of dollars; (c) Edward will easily be found at fault, especially since his phone records will show that he was sending a text or e-mail at the time of the wreck; and (d) the lawsuit judgment could be hundreds of thousands—or even millions—of dollars. Both Edward and his employer, the construction company, will be on the hook for the damages because an employer is responsible for the actions of its employees. So if the construction company does not have adequate insurance coverage, there is a good chance the company's assets will be used to pay part of the judgment, and it could bankrupt the company.

In sum, Edward's actions of driving while texting or e-mailing have a high "legal risk" because he could cause catastrophic harm, for which he would easily be found liable, and the damages could easily exceed his employer's insurance-coverage limits—and in that event, Edward's employer would have to pay over its money and assets to satisfy the claim. Plus, as will be explained in chapter 4, it is possible that the construction company's insurance may not apply at all … leaving the construction company with no alternative but to pay the entire liability out of its assets or file bankruptcy.

"Edward" is not entirely fictional ... According to an arrest warrant issued in 2014 by the Cobb County Georgia Police Department, a woman was arrested in connection with a March 10, 2014 crash in Austell, Georgia, which killed a thirty-six-year-old basketball coach. According to the arrest warrant, the woman got a text message on her phone right before the crash but deleted it before letting police see her phone. The arrest warrant also states that the woman "received multiple phone calls and placed a phone call at the time of the collision."

You must assess the activities in which you engage and determine your legal risks—and not just *your* activities but also those undertaken by other people for whom you can be held legally responsible. The largest group of people whose actions you may be legally responsible for are your employees. You can also be held liable for the actions of your minor children. You have the ability to control your actions, but you do not have the ability to control the actions of your employees. Businesses have been saddled with tremendous liabilities due to the actions of employees.

If the legal risks of such activities are moderate or high, you must take action—and that action is comprehensive asset-protection planning.

Can you be held responsible for the acts of others?

ABSOLUTELY!

You can be held legally responsible for the acts of your *employees* and *minor children* and, possibly, your *independent contractors*.

Below is a tiny sampling of recent lawsuits decided by Georgia courts that illustrate the legal risks of different activities and the size of the judgments against individuals and businesses in the state. The lawsuits are categorized by the type of activity. The activities are ones in which many people engage on a daily basis. We did not select lawsuits that only a small portion of Georgians undertake, such as driving a semitruck. We also tried not to select cases where the person's behavior was outrageous—for example, someone who leads police on a high-speed automobile chase through downtown Savannah on a Wednesday morning. These cases illustrate how ordinary people can become liable for large amounts of money if they do not assess the legal risks of their activities and undertake comprehensive asset-protection planning.

1. Lawsuit by a tenant who rented a residence from a landlord; the legal-risk activity is renting residential property to tenants.

a. Court verdict: $5,050,000. A tenant was injured and eventually died from injuries suffered when the deck of her rental home collapsed. In 2012, a DeKalb County court ruled that the landlord/owner of the house was liable.

b. Court verdict: $1,000,000. A tenant claimed she gave her landlord notice that her roof was leaking. The landlord

> **Hudson's Tip:** Owning residential rental property has a high legal risk. Often, the tenant and the property owner are not on friendly terms. As discussed in chapter 10, having (1) a written lease that is favorable to the landlord, (2) the property owned by an LLC, (3) debt on the property, and (4) proper liability insurance are Georgia Comprehensive Asset Protection Planning steps.

did not make the repair. The roof collapsed and injured the tenant. In 2013, a DeKalb County court ruled that that landlord/owner was liable.

c. Court verdict: $2,000,000. A tenant was attacked and injured at her apartment. The tenant claimed that her apartment complex was at fault for failing to provide adequate security to the tenants. In 2014, a DeKalb County court ruled that the apartment complex and its management group were liable.

2. Lawsuit by a customer who goes to a business to purchase goods or services; the legal-risk activity is inviting people to come onto your property to purchase goods and services.

> **Hudson's Tip:** As discussed in chapter 10, if you own the land and building where your business is located, it may be prudent to have one entity own the real estate and a different, separate entity own and operate the business.

a. Court verdict: $2,400,000. A man and his wife were guests at a small, popular resort in Georgia. The man became ill after his stay at the resort, and it was determined that the hot tub in his room contained the bacteria found in Legionnaires' Disease. The man died. In 2010, the US District Court for the Northern District of Georgia ruled that the resort was liable.

b. Court verdict: $5,000,000. A lady fell when entering a popular sporting goods store. She claimed that a sloping portion of the sidewalk was unpainted so as to warn her of the change in slope. The lady claimed that the sporting goods store was aware of the condition (or "on notice") since she was the third person who had tripped and fallen on the unpainted sidewalk. In 2010, a Fulton County court ruled that the sporting goods store was liable.

c. Court verdict: $1,500,000. A man was injured when he was in a popular home-improvement/hardware store and a pallet of plywood fell from the shelving and injured him. The man claimed that the store was negligent in creating a dangerous and unsafe environment. In 2009, a Cobb County court ruled that the store was liable.

3. Lawsuit by a person injured as a guest at your house; the legal-risk activity is inviting people to your home.

a. Court verdict: $700,000. The mother of an eight-year-old boy sued her neighbor claiming that the neighbor's pit bull attacked and severely injured the boy while playing in the neighbor's yard. The mother claimed that the neighbor knew of the dog's violent tendencies and failed to prevent the dog from attacking the boy. In 2011, a Douglas County court ruled that the neighbor was liable.

> *Hudson's Tip:* Homeowners may be liable for injuries sustained by their guests. Most homeowner insurance policies have some coverage for injuries to others; however, the coverage may not be sufficient or, as explained in Chapter 4, there may be an exclusion in the policy that eliminates the coverage. Review your policy!

b. Court verdict: $1,300,000. The parents of a young boy sued their neighbor claiming the boy fell in the neighbor's koi pond. The parents claimed that the pond was not surrounded by a fence and no signs were posted. The boy suffered severe brain damage. In 2009, a Fulton County court ruled that the neighborhood was liable.

c. Court verdict: $750,000. A lady sued her friend when she was invited over to the friend's house and tripped and fell over a crack in the sidewalk on the friend's property. The lady claimed she was injured. The lady claimed that the friend did not provide adequate lighting or warning of the dangerous premises. In 2012, a DeKalb County court ruled that the friend was liable.

4. Lawsuit by a person injured by an employee, and the employer was held liable; the legal-risk activity is having employees perform tasks that can cause serious injury.

Hudson's Tip: In Georgia, an employer is responsible for the actions of an employee when the employee acts within the scope of his or her employment. This can create a danger for a business that asks employees to use their autos to run errands or perform tasks that could cause injury to others. So if the employee causes an auto accident while running an errand for the employer, the employer can be liable! Use a courier service instead.

a. Court verdict: $3,150,000. The family of a bicycle rider claimed that the rider was struck by dump truck and killed. The estate of the bicycle rider claimed that the driver of the truck—an employee—was negligent, and that the truck driver's employer was vicariously liable for the injury because the driver was acting within the scope of employment at the time of the accident. In 2006, a Fulton County court ruled that the employer was liable.

b. Court verdict: $3,083,000. A pregnant woman claimed that she was injured when another car struck her vehicle, causing her baby to be born prematurely and die within a month. The woman claimed that because the driver of the car that hit hers was driving his car for business purposes of a company, the company was liable for the injuries. In 2013, a Bryan County court held the company/employer liable for the actions of its employee.

c. Court verdict: $5,662,759. An employee of a business claimed that he was unloading containers from his truck when another employee hit the truck with a vehicle, throwing the first employee to the ground where he sustained injuries. In 2012, a Chatham County court held that the employer was liable for the actions of the other employee.

d. Court verdict: $5,250,000. The mother of three children claimed that her children were killed in a house fire when the relief valve of a one-hundred-pound propane cylinder being stored in the basement failed and subsequently exploded. It was claimed that the retail-store attendant who filled the tank did not check for a required certification tag, which is contrary to Georgia law and the employee's yearly training from the propane supplier. The children's mother sued the store and the propane company. In 2004, a Fulton County court held the store liable for the actions of its employee.

5. Lawsuit by a person injured in an automobile accident; the legal-risk activity is driving an automobile.

a. Court verdict: $3,400,000. A lady claimed

> **Hudson's Tip:** Everyone who drives a car is taking part in a high-risk activity. Electronic devices such as telephones, laptops, navigation screens, and videos send the message that "driving is not a big deal, relax, and do another activity." Recently, I was on I-16 between Macon and Dublin and saw a man driving a big truck, traveling at eighty miles per hour, with a laptop on top of his steering wheel! In addition to having the socks sued off you, you could cause serious injury or death to someone. Put down the devices!

she was driving her car with her husband and daughter as passengers when a car driven by a man struck her car, and her husband and daughter were killed. The lady contended that the other driver failed to keep a proper lookout and his speeding was negligent. In 2005, a Gordon County court held the defendant driver liable.

b. Court verdict: $3,294,456. It was claimed that a married couple's car overturned after swerving to avoid hitting another car that swerved into their lane unexpectedly. The husband and wife were severely injured as a result. In 2010, a DeKalb County court held the other driver liable.

c. Reported settlement: $1,000,000. A lady's family claimed that she was killed in a car crash when a man driving another car ran into her lane. It was claimed that the other driver was speeding. In 2013, it was reported that the parties settled the case.

6. Lawsuit by an employee against the employer for injuries sustained by another employee while working; the legal-risk activity is having employees.

a. Court verdict: $4,553,028. An employee claimed he suffered severe burns when a steel barrel exploded on him at work. It was claimed that the employer failed to label the barrels for the safety of its employees. In 2001, the US District Court for the Northern District of Georgia held the employer liable.

b. Court verdict: $13,400,000. The family of an employee for an

> **Hudson's Tip:** When your employees are on the job, your business can be liable for their actions. Do background checks, drug tests, train employees on a regular basis, and hire only safe and responsible employees to help lower the risks.

apartment complex claimed that the employee was murdered in her apartment when a coworker (also an employee of the complex) entered her apartment without her permission. The victim's estate claims that the apartment-complex employer was negligent in its hiring practices and failed to run background checks on its employees before hiring them. In 2002, a Gwinnett County court held the employer liable.

NOTE: In chapter 10, the use of background checks of employees and people you do business with (babysitters, tenants, tutors for children, lawn-service companies, partners, vendors, etc.) is discussed.

c. Court verdict: $200,000. An employee sued his employer when the employee slipped on a bent step at his job and sustained injuries. The employee claimed his employer failed to keep the premises in a safe working condition. In 2012, the US District Court for the Middle District of Georgia held the employer liable.

7. Lawsuit by a client against the attorney for damages from bad legal service or advice; the legal-risk activity is practicing law.

a. Court verdict: $878,000. Clients sued their attorney and claimed that they lost a property due to their attorney failing

Hudson's Tip: An attorney who specializes in defending legal malpractice claims recently told me that 25 percent of Georgia lawyers do not have malpractice insurance. While conscientious professionals try not to err, everyone can make mistakes. All attorneys should have malpractice insurance to protect their assets and to protect their clients. Compared to medical malpractice insurance, legal malpractice insurance is inexpensive.

to prepare documents securing their deeded property. The clients claimed that the negligent act of the attorney forced the clients to file bankruptcy. In 2010, a Forsyth County court held the attorney liable.

b. Court verdict: $293,000. Clients sued their attorney and claimed they lost a great deal of money due to the attorney's negligence when advising them on a business transaction. In 2010, a Cherokee County court held the attorney liable.

c. Court verdict: $991,500. A client claimed legal malpractice against the attorney appointed to his case by his insurance company. The man had been involved in an accident and a lawsuit was brought against him. It was claimed that the lawyer admitted his client's guilt to the court without ever speaking to the client and a judgment was entered against the client. In 2007, a Gwinnett County court held the attorney liable.

d. Undisclosed $ settlement. A case that made the newspapers involved the prestigious King & Spalding law firm. It was reported that the law firm settled a $194.5 million malpractice suit filed by Atlanta Spirit, the company that owned the Atlanta Hawks professional basketball team and the Atlanta Thrashers professional ice-hockey team. Terms of the settlement, as is the case with many settlements, are confidential. Atlanta Spirit claimed that their attorney, employed by King & Spalding, drafted a contract that was "fatally flawed" because it prevented the Atlanta Spirit from selling the Thrashers at its own will. Atlanta Spirit sought $14.5 million in litigation expenses, $50 million for a loss in franchise value for the Thrashers, and reimbursement of $130 million in operating costs for the hockey team. The suit was finally dismissed in December 2010 when the parties settled the attorney malpractice claim out of court.

8. Lawsuit by a patient against the doctor for damages from medical malpractice; the legal-risk activity is practicing medicine.

a. Court verdict: $1,265,000. A patient sued her plastic surgeon, claiming that the doctor performed a face-lift on her and her skin began to die and deteriorate as a result of the procedure, leaving her permanently disfigured. In 2008, a Fulton County court held the doctor liable.

> **Hudson's Tip:** One benefit of having quality medical malpractice insurance is that the insurance company will hire and pay for lawyers who specialize in defending the claims of patients and in dealing with lawyers who sue doctors. The Georgia Supreme Court recently held that the cap on noneconomic damages in medical malpractices cases is unconstitutional.

b. Court verdict: $9,217,000. A patient's estate claimed a doctor incorrectly diagnosed the patient with food poisoning and sent him home when in fact the man suffered from an undiagnosed peptic ulcer. The man died hours after leaving the doctor. In 2004, a Fulton County court held the doctor liable.

c. Court verdict: $3,000,000. A patient's family claimed a doctor overrode an order to administer only 2 mg of morphine and gave the patient ten times that amount. The patient died. In 2009, a Dougherty County court held the doctor liable.

9. Lawsuit by a person injured by an intoxicated driver after the driver was served alcohol while visibly intoxicated and about to operate a motor vehicle; the legal-risk activity is serving alcohol and permitting an intoxicated guest to drive.

a. Court verdict: $1,000,000. It was claimed that a restaurant served a visibly intoxicated customer who subsequently drove his vehicle and was involved in an auto accident that resulted in fatalities. A Cobb County court held the restaurant owner liable.

b. Court verdict: $300,000. It was claimed that a man provided alcohol to his girlfriend who was visibly intoxicated and the man knew that his girlfriend was going to operate a vehicle in the near future. Further, it was claimed that the girlfriend drove her vehicle and injured another person in a car accident. In 2007, a Gwinnett County court held the man who served the alcohol to his girlfriend liable.

> **Hudson's Tip:** Georgia's Dram Shop and Social Host Liability laws impose liability on people who knowingly sell or furnish alcohol to customers (or guests/friends in your home) who are visibly intoxicated, knowing that the person will soon be driving a motor vehicle. Most companies have stopped serving alcohol at company functions for this reason.

c. Court verdict: $325,000. It was claimed that after a restaurant served alcohol to a noticeably intoxicated patron, the patron caused a car accident, and others were injured. In 2010, the US District Court for the Middle District of Georgia held the restaurant liable.

10. Lawsuits against the parent of a minor child who injured another person; the legal-risk activity is permitting minor children to do things that can cause injury to others.

a. Court verdict: $1,937,000. A woman claimed that a sixteen-year-old driver was at fault in an automobile accident where she was injured. The woman claimed that the parents of the sixteen-year-old are liable through the family purpose doctrine. In 2009, a Cobb County court held the parents liable for negligently entrusting the vehicle to a minor.

b. Court verdict: $500,327. It was claimed that a teenager rear-ended another car while driving his mother's car. The driver of the other vehicle claimed he was injured and claimed that the teenager's mother was liable through the family purpose doctrine. In 2009, a Fulton County court held the mother liable for failure to exercise ordinary care in letting her son drive the family car.

c. Reported settlement: $440,000. A passenger in a car claimed that his seventeen-year-old friend crashed an SUV owned by the seventeen-year-old's parents. The passenger friend was injured. The passenger and his parents claimed that the parents of the minor driver were liable under the family purpose doctrine, because the SUV belonged to the parents. In 2000, a trial was held in Fulton County, and after one day, the parties reportedly agreed to settle the case for $440,000 in favor of the passenger (presumably he was no longer a friend of the seventeen-year-old driver).

> *Hudson's Tip:* You can be liable for the actions of minor children. Make certain that your insurance agent knows that your child should be added to your liability policies. Teach your children by example: *Do not text, e-mail, or use a cell phone while you are driving.* Show your children that it is not acceptable to drive after you have consumed alcohol; don't drive if you have had *any* alcohol.

11. Lawsuits against an engineer/architect for damages caused by faulty design; the legal-risk activity is performing engineering and architectural services.

a. Court verdict: $1,421,120. Homeowners sued an engineering firm that constructed a retention pond for a supermarket next to their house. The homeowners claimed that the negligent construction and maintenance of the pond destroyed their land by flooding it. In 2010, a Hall County court held the engineering firm liable to the homeowners.

> **Hudson's Tip:** Engineers and architects can be held liable to people other than their clients; they can also be held liable by people who are injured from their designs and products.

b. Court verdict: $5,580,000. A condo developer claimed that an engineering firm was negligent in the design and engineering of the sanitary/storm drain systems, which in turn flooded and destroyed the condo complex. In 2006, a Fulton County court held the engineering firm liable.

c. Court verdict: $2,200,000. It was claimed that a defective airbag resulted in the death of a woman while driving her minivan. The woman's estate claimed professional negligence against the engineers at the auto manufacturer for defective design and assembly. In 2009, the District Court for the Northern District of Georgia held the automaker and its engineers liable.

12. Lawsuits by an injured party against a business that provided a service to a customer and the customer was not the injured party; the legal-risk activity is providing services to the public.

a. Court verdict: $2,575,000. A lady visited a vacant home listed for sale on the Internet. The lady fell ten feet to the ground when the deck collapsed and nearly severed her foot. The lady sued the management company that inspected the deck. In 2007, a Fulton County court held the inspection company liable.

b. Court verdict: $3,570,610. A general contractor engaged a subcontractor to install a fireplace for a homeowner. The homeowner sued the subcontractor (the fireplace-installation company) claiming that the fireplace ignited and started a fire. The subcontractor had no contract with the homeowner, only with the general contractor. In 2012, a Cobb County court held the subcontractor liable.

> **Hudson's Tip:** Your liability is not limited to the persons with whom you directly contract. In Georgia, you can be held liable for injuries to all persons that could "foreseeably" be injured by your work.

c. Court verdict: $1,400,000. A woman riding on an escalator at a MARTA station in Atlanta claimed she was thrown off of the escalator and was injured when the escalator began to move in reverse very quickly. The woman sued MARTA and also the escalator-inspection company, which had a contract with MARTA to install, inspect, and maintain the escalators. A Fulton County court held the escalator-inspection company 55 percent at fault for negligent repair and inspection.

CHAPTER 3 RECAP:

1. There are hundreds of thousands of lawsuits filed in Georgia each year, and people and businesses with money are targets. Just look at the billboards and TV commercials by attorneys looking for the next $1 million case.

2. Everyone can make mistakes, and the financial consequences can be staggering. An activity that all of us perform—driving a car—could cause injury and great financial harm. Add another activity like talking on the phone, texting, or e-mailing while driving, and the possibility of being at fault spikes!

3.   Business owners are liable for their own actions and can also be liable for the actions of their employees, and sometimes independent contractors.

4.   Georgia courts have rendered very big verdicts against individuals and businesses who were involved in an accident or who were legally responsible for someone else (like a child or employee) who caused an accident.

CHAPTER 4

LIABILITY INSURANCE IS NOT ENOUGH

Liability insurance is intended to pay for the harm and damage that you cause to another person and that person's property. Many people who live in Georgia have purchased liability insurance. In Georgia, you are required to have liability insurance to drive a car.

An important step in protecting your assets should be the purchase of quality liability insurance from a reputable insurance company and an experienced insurance agent. Why should you do this instead of buying the cheapest liability insurance available? Because you want a company that is going to take prompt action to address a claim against you; you don't want a company that is going to do everything it can to avoid paying a claim against you.

However, even having a liability insurance policy from a good and reputable insurance company will not prevent a court judgment against you that exceeds the coverage amount of your insurance. If the insurance company does not pay all of the claim against you, *you* are going to have to pay the remainder of the claim out of *your* assets.

For example, in the automobile cases cited in chapter 3, the courts awarded the injured persons the following amounts: $3,400,000; $3,294,456; and $1,000,000. Most people do not have automobile liability insurance coverage that would cover those awards. So the first reason liability insurance is not sufficient to protect your assets is that the liability against you may exceed the insurance coverage.

The second reason that liability insurance may not protect your money and assets is something called a "coverage exclusion." This is a clause in an insurance policy that essentially nullifies the coverage. To be more specific, coverage exclusions provide that the insurance company does not have to pay in the event of certain events or behavior. For example, many liability policies do not cover damage to property or injury to a person if you intentionally cause the damage or injury; so, if you get mad at someone and *intentionally* punch them in the nose, your insurance will not cover the damage to the other person's nose. If, however, you *accidentally* fall and injure someone, that injury will likely be covered.

I have never seen a liability insurance policy that does not contain exclusions. I spend a lot of money each year for liability insurance coverage, and I believe that I have high-quality insurance policies. My professional liability policy, homeowners policy, automobile insurance, commercial insurance policy,

> You must also audit your liability policies. Your insurance policies *must* be reviewed and the exclusions examined. Insurance policies issued by one company are different from policies issued by other companies. A large portion of liability insurance policies address what is *not* covered—the exclusions! You should review your homeowner's insurance policy, commercial liability insurance policy, automobile insurance policy, professional liability policy, etc. and read the exclusions.

and umbrella insurance policy all contain coverage exclusions. Your policies contain exclusions, too, and if you do not know what the exclusions are, then you do not know the extent to which your policies are giving you protection.

The third reason that liability insurance may not be sufficient to protect your assets involves timeliness. If you fail to "timely" notify your insurance company that someone has a claim against you, your insurance company can deny coverage. In fact, Georgia has a law, Section 33–7–15, that provides with respect to automobile insurance that if someone files a lawsuit against you—and the sheriff serves the lawsuit on you—you must "timely" notify the insurance company of the lawsuit, or the insurance company does not have to pay for the claim. Most insurance policies require that you notify your insurance company "as soon as practical" after you learn that someone has or might have a claim against you.

> *Hudson's Tip:* Some people do not want to report an accident to their insurance company because the insurance company will either increase the premium or cancel the policy. This can be a dangerous strategy. Recently, I hit another car as I was backing out of a parking space. The other car was damaged and it was my fault. The occupants of the other car were not hurt and were very nice and friendly. I immediately reported the accident to my insurance company and gave all the particulars including that I thought it was my fault. Sometime later, my insurance company called me to let me know that the people were now claiming that they had suffered "personal injuries." My premium did increase as a result of the accident, but what if I had not notified my insurance company "as soon as practical" and the insurance company denied coverage? I would have had to hire a lawyer at a cost much higher than my increased premium to fight the claim that the people suffered personal injuries!

The fourth reason that liability insurance is not sufficient to protect your assets is that you may get sued for something that is not covered by liability insurance. You may get sued by someone who claims that you breached a contract and therefore owe him or her money. Most contract claims are not covered by liability insurance.

Have you ever added up the premiums that you pay every year for liability insurance? Most people have purchased their liability insurance policies from different companies and agents. For example, most people have the same agent for their homeowners and automobile policies, but have a different agent for their general liability insurance, another agent for their professional insurance, and yet another for their property and casualty insurance. Your various agents probably do not talk to each other and have not looked at your other policies. You have a patchwork of policies and hope to goodness that all of your agents are great. A better approach is to have *one* person look at all of your policies and review your coverages to make sure that you are not overpaying, to make sure that your coverages are proper for your legal risks, and to advise you of the exclusions and items your policies do not cover. Only then can you intelligently undertake the other phases of Georgia Comprehensive Asset Protection Planning.

Below is a sampling of cases decided by Georgia courts holding that an insurance company did not have to pay a claim under a liability policy because of an exclusion in the policy. The cases are categorized by the type of liability coverage. Also included below are notes on exclusions for the specific types of policies.

1. Exclusions in automobile liability insurance policies.
  a. Coverage exclusion for regularly using another car (2008). A lady was involved in an automobile accident while driving her friend's car. The lady's insurance company claimed that the following exclusion

in her policy relieved the insurance company from liability:

> "We will not pay for any damages a person insured [the lady] is legally obligated to pay because of … a nonowned auto, which is furnished or available for the regular use of a person insured [the lady]."

The Georgia Court of Appeals held in favor of the insurance company.

b. Coverage exclusion for failure to list son on application (2012). It was claimed that a lady's son accidentally struck and injured a pedestrian with the family car. The pedestrian sued the mother and son. The mother notified her automobile insurance company, but the company said that it was not responsible for the claim due to following exclusion in the mother's policy:

> "We will not provide coverage for any claim arising from an accident or loss involving a motorized vehicle being operated by a household resident who, at the time of the application, was not listed on the application but who operated a vehicle listed on the application."

Common Automobile Insurance Exclusions

1. Property of the insured
2. Bodily injury to a family member
3. Willful or intentional injury
4. Injury to employees of insured
5. Injuries to fellow employees of insured
6. Business use
7. Nonowned automobile furnished for regular use
8. Unlisted drivers
9. Unlawful act or traffic violation

The Georgia Court of Appeals held in favor of the insurance company; since the mother failed to list her son as a driver on the application, the exclusion applied.

2. Exclusions in homeowners liability insurance policies

a. Coverage exclusion for intentional conduct (2009). It was claimed that a homeowner punched and injured a man during an altercation on the homeowner's property. The injured man filed suit against the homeowner. The homeowner's insurance company denied coverage because the policy contained an exclusion for "intended injuries," providing that there would be no coverage for behavior dealing with injuries that were expected or intended by the insured. The Georgia Court of Appeals held in favor of the insurance company because the homeowner's act of punching the man was intentional and the exclusion applied.

> **Common Homeowners Policy Exclusions**
>
> 1. Mold damage
> 2. Flood/water damage
> 3. Aggressive dog breeds
> 4. Neglect to home repairs
> 5. Sewage backup
> 6. ATVs used off premises
> 7. Power-outage surges
> 8. Intentional damage by resident
> 9. Trampolines and swimming pools

Note: Liability insurance is generally intended to cover accidents and mistakes (lawyers call this "negligence"). Intentional acts, such as punching someone in the nose, are often excluded from insurance policies.

b. Coverage exclusion for recreational vehicle (1996). It was claimed that a nine-year-old girl was driving a minibike with her minor friend as a passenger. Even though the minibike was not intended for road usage, the girls were driving on a public roadway. A car struck the minibike and the passenger/friend on the minibike was injured. The mother of the passenger/friend sued the parents of the nine-year-old. The parents' insurance company denied coverage. The policy had an exclusion for motor vehicles intended for recreational use while off of the insured's property. The Georgia Court of Appeals held in favor of the insurance company; the exclusion applied.

c. Coverage exclusion for all-terrain vehicles (2009). Home-owners held a sixteenth birthday party for their daughter. During the party, the homeowners' daughter and her friend were involved in an accident on a four-wheeler in a field next to the homeowners' property. The friend was injured and the homeowners were sued. The homeowners' insurance company said an exclusion barred recovery for incidents involving "all-terrain vehicles when they are used away from the insured premises." Finding that the field where the girls were injured was not a "premises used by an insured person in connection with the residence premises," the Georgia Court of Appeals held that the insurance company did not have to cover the damages.

d. Homeowners' insurer rescinded coverage when notified of diving board and trampoline on premises (2009). Homeowners filled out an insurance application and notified the insurer that they had a swimming pool, diving board, and trampoline on their property. The insurance company notified the homeowners that they would not be able to cover them due to the existence of the diving board and trampoline. The homeowners then removed the diving board and sent pictures to the insurer and agreed to an endorsement excluding coverage for injuries caused on the trampoline. Contingent upon the removal of the diving board and the agreement of the trampoline exclusion, the insurance company issued a policy to the homeowners. After being issued the policy, the homeowners reinstalled the diving board. When a tornado damaged the property, an agent was sent out to assess the property damage and noticed that the diving board had been reinstalled. The insurer brought a claim against the homeowner for material misrepresentations during the application process.

A Henry County court held that the insurance company was not liable for *any* property damage due to the material misrepresentations made by the homeowners. The Georgia Court of Appeals affirmed this ruling.

> *Hudson's Tip:* Tell only the truth, especially on an insurance application (whether it be for health, life, or liability insurance) because the insurance company likely will be able to deny paying for a claim if you have been less than truthful.

3. Exclusions in commercial general liability policies—a business gets sued and the insurance company says there is no coverage

a. Coverage exclusion for serving alcohol (2001). It was claimed that a café served alcohol to a noticeably intoxicated patron, who then drove her vehicle and collided with another car and driver.

When the café was sued, the general liability insurance company informed the café that the following "alcohol-distribution exclusion" relieved the company of responsibility:

"This policy does not apply … to bodily injury … due to the sale or distribution of alcohol."

The Georgia Court of Appeals held that the café's activity of serving the patron while she was noticeably intoxicated fell within the scope of the exclusion, and therefore the insurance company had no duty to pay.

b. Coverage exclusion for injury from automobile (2001). A man owned a logging business. One of his trucks was involved in an auto accident with a lady and two children, where the lady and her two children suffered injuries. The logging business was sued. The general liability insurance company for the logging business denied coverage because of an "automobile exception" in its policy, barring recovery for bodily injury stemming from a motor vehicle owned by the company. The Georgia Court of Appeals held in favor of the insurance company.

Common General Commercial Liability Policy Exclusions

1. Expected or intended injury

2. Liquor liability

3. Pollution/fungus or asbestos

4. Automobile use

5. Nuclear/chemical material

6. Professional negligence

7. Employee injury/worker's compensation

8. Aircraft, auto, or watercraft

9. Damage to "your work"

10. Product recall

11. Negligent hiring/supervision

12. Business pursuits

13. Punitive damages

c. Coverage exclusion for subcontracted work (2004). A general contractor hired a subcontractor to perform a portion of the work on a residential construction project. The subcontractor damaged the residence, and the homeowners sued the general contractor. The general contractor's insurance company claimed that it was not required to defend the suit based on a "your work" exclusion, which barred recovery for work that was improperly done by the general contractor, *or any subcontractor* that he may have hired, which subsequently must be repaired. The Georgia Court of Appeals held that the "your work" exclusion applied, and the insurance company was not required to defend the suit.

d. Coverage exclusion for negligent hiring (1998). An employee was involved in a car accident with a third party, and the third party sued the employee's employer. The claim was that the employer negligently hired and retained the employee. The employer's liability insurer asserted that the automobile-accident exclusion eliminated coverage for the claims of negligent hiring and retention. The Georgia Court of Appeals held for the insurance company.

e. Coverage exclusion for "Your Work" (2000). It was claimed that an employee injured himself on a stone-cutting saw that was designed and manufactured by his employer to be sold to a specific customer. The employee sued his employer because the saw did not have a guard to protect the blade. The employer's liability insurer claimed that the "products completed operations hazard" exclusion applied. The policy provided:

> "This insurance does not apply ... to bodily injury ... arising out of 'your work' or 'your product' when it has been deemed completed."

The Georgia Court of Appeals held for the insurance company; the exclusion applied.

f. Coverage exclusion for "Your Defective Work" (2010). A grading company hired a contracting company to do some work. The grading company claimed that the contractor produced defective work product. The contracting company's insurance company claimed that the following "business risks" exclusion applied:

> "Business-risk exclusions ... are designed to exclude coverage for defective workmanship by the insured builder causing damage to the construction project itself."

The Georgia Court of Appeals held for the insurance company, agreeing that the exclusion applied. Thus, the contracting company would be liable for any cost of repair that the grading company incurred.

g. Coverage exclusion for emotional harm caused by sexual harassment (1996). A woman brought a sexual-harassment suit against her employer claiming that her office manager made numerous inappropriate gestures and advances. The employer's general liability provider claimed the harm alleged did not fall within the policy coverage. The insurer asserted that it was only liable for bodily injury, property damage, personal injury, and advertising injury, and that the emotional harm caused to the employee "does not fall within the bodily injury category," because there was no physical harm to the employee. The Georgia Court of Appeals held for the insurance company.

h. Coverage exclusion for assault by an employee (1998). An employee of a nightclub attacked a man in the parking lot of the business, and the victim sued the nightclub. The nightclub's insurance company claimed that it was not required to defend the case, based on an assault-and-battery exclusion in the policy. The Georgia Court of Appeals held for the insurance company.

4. Exclusions in Professional Liability Policies.

a. Coverage exclusion for dishonest conduct (1996). It was claimed that one partner in a law firm improperly withdrew funds from a client's escrow account for personal use. The client sued the law firm to recover the money. The law firm sought coverage from its professional liability insurance policy for the client's claim. The insurance company claimed that an exclusion applied for acts arising out of "dishonest, fraudulent, or criminal and malicious conduct." The Georgia Supreme Court held for the insurance company; the partner's action *did* arise out of the excluded type of conduct, and therefore fell within the scope of the exclusion.

b. Coverage exclusion for sexual misconduct (1995). A woman claimed that her psychologist sexually assaulted her while she was under hypnosis. She brought suit against the doctor, and his malpractice insurer asked the court to determine its liability based on an "improper-sexual-misconduct" exclusion. The Superior Court of Bibb County found that the malpractice insurer had no duty to defend the suit because

---

Common Professional-Liability Policy Exclusions

1. Bodily injury
2. Property damage
3. Fraudulent acts
4. Employment matters
5. Patents & trade secrets
6. Use of drugs or alcohol
7. Services rendered outside of specialty
8. Incidents prior to coverage

---

the exclusion applied and was not void as a matter of public policy. Therefore, the insurer did not defend the suit and the doctor was liable for all damages that arose from the malpractice suit.

> **Note:** Below are common exclusions found in most medical-malpractice policies.
>
> - liability for any claim made against an insured prior to the effective date of the policy, or any claim arising from an incident made known to the insurer or prior insurer before the effective date of the policy
> - liability for any claim arising from an incident that took place prior to the retroactive date of the policy
> - liability arising from fraudulent or malicious acts intended to cause harm; criminal acts; violation of any statute, code, ordinance, or regulation; unfair business practices; violation of any consumer protection law; or violation of any civil-rights law
> - liability arising from an insured person's abuse of or being under the influence of alcohol, drugs, or any other substance
> - liability arising out of an insured person's guarantee of the results of professional services
> - liability resulting from any professional services that an insured person renders outside of his or her specialty, as listed on the policy documents and as limited by his or her representations in any application for insurance

5. Exclusions in umbrella policies.

a. **Coverage exclusion in personal umbrella policy for off-road vehicles (2012).** This action arose out of the 2009 case discussed earlier in this chapter, where a sixteen-year-old girl and her friend were riding a four-wheeler on property adjacent to the home. We learned that the parents' homeowners policy would not defend the case based on an exclusion in the policy for "off-road vehicles used away from the insured's premises." The parents then asked their umbrella insurance provider to defend the suit. The umbrella insurer claimed that an exclusion applied in its policy for "use of *any* motorized vehicle designed for off-road use," which would include a four-wheeler. The Georgia Court of Appeals held for the insurance company.

Common Umbrella Policy Exclusions

1. Expected or intended injury

2. Business or professional pursuits

3. Auto, air, or watercraft use

4. Use of most recreational vehicles

5. Business-related injuries

6. Nonrelated persons

7. Criminal acts or DUI

8. Professional malpractice

---

b. Coverage exclusion in personal umbrella policy for non-related persons (1996). Defendant was driving a friend's car, with the friend's permission, and caused an accident with a motorcyclist. The motorcyclist sued the driver of the car. The driver was covered under the car owner's liability policy as a permitted driver, but the policy limit was $100,000, and the damages exceeded that amount. The motorcyclist tried to force the car owner's umbrella policy to pay out. The insurance company claimed the following exclusion in the umbrella policy:

> "The policy only covers harm to the insured and any persons related by blood or living with the insured."

The Georgia Court of Appeals held for the insurance company; the permissive driver and the motorcyclist were both excluded from recovery against the umbrella policy.

c. Coverage exclusion in commercial umbrella policy for intentional acts (1996). An employee brought a sexual-harassment claim against her employer, who notified his homeowner's and personal umbrella policy providers. The homeowner's insurance provider denied coverage based on an "intended acts" exclusion. The employer then addressed his umbrella insurer and received the same response. The umbrella policy had the following exclusion: "For acts intended to cause bodily harm, including mental anguish." The Georgia Court of Appeals held for the insurance company; the exclusion applied.

6. Denial of Coverage for Failure to Give "Timely" Notice to the Insurance Company of an "Occurrence."

In addition to exclusions for coverage, an insurance company can deny coverage if you do not notify the insurance company in a timely manner that someone has, or may have, a claim against you. Georgia, unlike many states, does not require that the insurance company be prejudiced or harmed by the failure to give notice in order to deny coverage.

The Georgia Supreme Court recently decided a failure-to-notify case that involved millions of dollars. An employee of a church was accused of sexually abusing the plaintiff, who said that the church was liable for its employee. The plaintiff sued the church, and seventeen months after the lawsuit was filed against the church, the church notified the insurance company. The insurance policy had a clause that said the church had to notify the insurance company of an "occurrence" as soon as practical. The notice provision further required the church to provide all details about the occurrence (where it happened, who was involved, names of witnesses, etc.). The court ruled that the insurance company did not have to pay the claim filed by the church. The church argued that even if its notice was not timely, the insurance company was not prejudiced or harmed by the late notice and still should be required to pay. The court disagreed, because in Georgia insurance companies do not need to be harmed; insurance companies can get out of coverage simply because of late notice.

CHAPTER 4 RECAP:

There are four reasons why the purchase of liability insurance is not sufficient to protect your assets:

1. A court judgment against you could be greater than your liability coverage.

2. Your policy may contain an exclusion so that you do not get insurance coverage.

3. If you do not notify the insurance company about the occurrence or accident in a timely manner, the insurance company can deny coverage.

4. The claim against you may be a contract claim, and liability insurance does not cover it.

All of your liability insurance policies should be audited to make sure that you are not overpaying for your insurance coverages and so that you know whether your legal risks are covered. Once the audit is complete, you can intelligently continue to engage in Georgia Comprehensive Asset Protection Planning.

C H A P T E R 5

FRAUDULENT TRANSFERS: DON'T GET CAUGHT MAKING ONE!

"Hey, I have a great idea … listen … once it is clear that I owe someone a lot of money, I will simply give my assets to my spouse, children or friends! Or here's an even better idea, I will sell my real estate to my brother for a promissory note that he does not pay for twenty years and he will give the property back to me for free if I ask him." Bad ideas … those are fraudulent transfers.

Georgia has a set of laws that prevents a person from transferring an asset with the intent of trying to defeat a creditor from collecting on a claim. A "creditor" is a person who has a "claim." "Claim" is very broadly defined to mean a right to payment, whether or not the right is (a) reduced to judgment, (b) fixed, (c) contingent, or (d) disputed.

So, if Larry rear-ends another driver while he is sending a text message or otherwise not paying attention, and the other driver is seriously injured and taken to the emergency room, that injured driver is a "creditor" … even though he or she has not yet filed a lawsuit against Larry. The injured party has a "claim" because he or she has a right to payment, since Larry was at fault—even though Larry's attorney may dispute the claim. If, a week after the accident, while still no lawsuit has been filed, Larry deeds his house and transfers all bank and stock accounts to his spouse, then the transfers that Larry made are classified as "fraudulent transfers."

If a "fraudulent transfer" is made, then the creditor (in the example above, the injured person who was rear-ended) can have a judge set aside or void the transfer.

The laws in Georgia that describe when a fraudulent transfer has been made and the rights of the parties are known as the Georgia Uniform Fraudulent Transfers Act (or the "GUFTA" for short). The GUFTA is a revised and updated set of laws that went into effect in 2002.

Before the GUFTA, Georgia had an earlier set of laws that addressed transfers by creditors made with the intent of defeating legitimate creditors. It is important to understand that, like some other states, Georgia has had a detailed set of rules or statutes that describe and address fraudulent transfers—for almost one hundred years! Because people who owe others money have been trying to get out of paying their debts for *more* than one hundred years.

Beginning with the great recession that started in 2008 and ended in 2011, a number of real estate developers and operators were referred to me from other lawyers for "asset-protection planning" … but that's not really what it was. These men and women owed millions and millions of dollars to banks. Almost all of them had loans that exceeded the value of the properties that secured them, so these folks were insolvent. Almost all of them wanted to make a transfer or gift to a trust for their children or directly to a relative or close friend or business associate. And almost all of them swore to me, with great conviction, that they would *never* personally guarantee a loan again and would do anything they could to stop anyone else from making such a mistake. But, alas, I was unable to assist most of these clients, because the transfers these men and women wished to make were classified as fradulent under the GUFTA. *The lesson, again, is that comprehensive asset-protection planning must be done in advance of trouble.*

In Appendix C, I've included a reprint of the GUFTA for those who want to read it. However, I submit that the GUFTA is a set of technical rules and definitions that codify and complicate the "smell test." In other words, if it smells fishy, it's a fraudulent transfer. And you do not need to be a lawyer to smell fish.

There are a couple of parts of the GUFTA that are worth noting: first, a nonexclusive list of "badges of fraud" (that is, actions that are suspicious); and, second, a time limit within which a creditor must make a claim that a debtor has made a fraudulent transfer.

Badges of fraud. Remember that a fraudulent transfer is one that is made with "intent" to frustrate a creditor. Direct proof of "intent" is rare. An example of direct proof is an e-mail from a debtor to his brother-in-law that details and admits to a scheme to frustrate a creditor. For example, that the debtor will transfer his bank and stock accounts to a new trust for his children, the brother-in-law will be the trustee of the trust and—after the creditor has gone away—the brother-in-law will dissolve the trust and transfer the assets back to the debtor. Many advisors tell debtors to be secret and never put the real plan in writing, so direct proof is rare to find. But to be sure, there are no secrets, because the brother-in-law, and probably others, know about the scheme. Is the brother-in-law going to lie in a courtroom?

The badges of fraud are a list of facts or circumstances that help measure or detect "intent." The full list of the badges of fraud can be found in Georgia Code Section 18–2–74(b).

BADGES OF FRAUD (Also Known As "Smelly Fish")

- The debtor transfers substantially all of his assets. (Think about it—other than submitting to a vow of poverty and joining a religious movement—why would someone transfer all or most of his or her assets?)

- The debtor has been sued or threatened with a lawsuit before the transfer.

- The transfer was made to a relative or business associate.

- The transfer was concealed or not disclosed.

- The transfer occurred shortly before or shortly after a substantial debt was incurred.

- The debtor retained control or possession of the property that was transferred.

- The transfer was made for less than reasonable value.

- The debtor was insolvent when the transfer was made or became insolvent shortly after the transfer was made.

GUFTA's Statute of Limitations. Perhaps the most important part of the GUFTA is the statute of limitations—that is, the time within which a creditor must assert that another person has engaged in a fraudulent transfer.

Georgia Code Section 18–2–79 provides that a cause of action by a creditor with respect to a fraudulent transfer is extinguished unless the action is brought within four years after the transfer was made or the obligation was incurred (or, if later, within one year after the transfer or obligation was or could reasonably have been discovered by the claimant).

So, if a debtor living in Atlanta deeds his house to his spouse, the deed is recorded in the Fulton County Superior Court land records (instead of sitting in the debtor's desk), the debtor discloses the transfer on his financial statements, and four years pass after the transfer, then a creditor should not be successful in asserting that the transfer was fraudulent under the GUFTA. The Fulton County land records are public records that can be viewed by anyone, so recording the deed was a public disclosure of the transfer.

Hudson's Tip: Disclosure helps suspicion evaporate.

Occasionally, when I represent the executor of a deceased person's estate, the client/executor complains that a beneficiary is being hostile. Often, the beneficiary has made a request for copies of bank-account statements or other financial statements of the deceased person, and the executor has told the beneficiary that he does not have to turn that information over to the beneficiary. Even though the executor may not be required to turn over the documents, what is the harm in giving the beneficiary the requested copies? In fact, I often advise my clients to give the beneficiary full access and opportunity to view all the financial records, as the beneficiary will most often conclude that, because there has been full disclosure, the executor is not hiding anything or doing anything incorrectly. The principle of disclosure works everywhere, including the GUFTA.

With comprehensive asset-protection planning, there is no need to hide— and there is no lying. It allows you to stay in front and out of trouble.

Below are summaries of several Georgia cases involving fraudulent transfers, which illustrate how the fraudulent-transfer laws are applied by Georgia courts and judges. The cases are divided into two groups: (1) cases where the debtor *had not* filed bankruptcy; and (2) cases where the debtor *had* filed bankruptcy. You will probably be able to correctly guess the outcome of each case just by learning the facts of the case.

When a Georgia resident or business entity files bankruptcy, the filing is made in a federal bankruptcy court, not a state court. The US Bankruptcy Code governs bankruptcies. Section 548 of the Bankruptcy Code describes and addresses fraudulent transfers—and under the Bankruptcy Code, these are very similar to fraudulent transfers under GUFTA. As an example, bankruptcy courts use a nonexclusive list of "badges of fraud" similar to the list under GUFTA.

1. Fraudulent-transfer cases where the debtor did not file bankruptcy.

a. Case in Catoosa County, Georgia; debtor tries to avoid child-support debt (2000). The debtor was divorced and required to make child-support payments to his ex-wife. The debtor stopped paying child support on numerous occasions. When he was notified by his ex-wife that he needed to pay her more than $9,000 in medical bills for their children, the debtor transferred all of his assets except for $225 to his then-girlfriend. The ex-wife brought suit to set aside the transfer because she believed it was fraudulent. The court set aside the transfer because, at the time of the transfer, the debtor was insolvent—meaning his debts outweighed his assets—and the transfer was made for no consideration.

b. Case in Muscogee County, Georgia; debtor tries to avoid a judgment with an unrecorded deed (2006). The debtor (a lawyer) signed a deed on December 1, 1999, to transfer property to his daughter, but he did not record the deed in the Muscogee County land records until May 25, 2001—one day after a judgment was entered against him. The debtor claimed that the conveyance of property was not fraudulent because he signed the transfer deed when he was still solvent. However, the debtor did not record the deed until years later when he was near (and would soon achieve) insolvency. The debtor claimed that the creditor's suit was barred under the GUFTA's statute of limitations because the lawsuit was filed more than four years after December 1, 1999—the date the debtor signed the unrecorded deed. The court held that (1) the date of the transfer was May 25, 2001 (the date the deed was recorded/disclosed), so the four-year statute of limitations had not run out, and (2) the transfer of property to the debtor's daughter was fraudulent because it was conveyed to an "insider" (defined by the GUFTA to include relatives) and the debtor continued to use the transferred property as his office, paid no rent to his daughter, and maintained complete control over the property.

> *Note:* This case was affirmed by the Georgia Supreme Court. If the court had allowed the date the unrecorded deed was signed to be the effective date of the transfer for purposes of the GUFTA's statute of limitations, all debtors would have a signed-but-unrecorded deed in their desk drawers! The court thought that would be ridiculous and did not want to encourage that kind of bogus behavior.

c. Case in Fulton County, Georgia (affirmed by Georgia Supreme Court); real estate developer and $19 million bank loan (2011). A bank made loans to corporations controlled by father and son residential-housing developers. Due to the housing-market decline, the borrowers defaulted on the loans. The bank investigated and learned that the father and son had created eight new limited liability companies and transferred over $330 million of the borrowers' assets to those new LLCs, leaving the borrowers with $25 million in assets. By the time the bank asked the court to freeze all transfers made by the father and son's companies, only $25,000 remained. The court granted the bank's interlocutory injunction, freezing the assets that had been fraudulently transferred.

> **Note:** In addition to the action under the GUFTA, the covenants in the borrowers' loan documents were also breached, and the bank sought relief under contract law, as well.

d. Case in bankruptcy court; debtor claims the reason for the transfers is estate planning (2009).

The debtor was suspected of violating Securities and Exchange Commission regulations. One day after a meeting with SEC investigators, the debtor transferred to his wife, by quitclaim deed, two pieces of real property, leaving himself with no substantial assets. The debtor claimed that the transfers were made for estate-planning purposes. At trial, the attorney who prepared the quitclaim deed

> **Hudson's Tip:** Estate planning is *not* an excuse to transfer assets fraudulently! Estate planning was not a very credible reason in this case, and it is going to be even less of a credible reason in the future, especially for transfers to a spouse. This is because the federal estate tax exemption was recently increased to over $5,490,000 per person so that a married couple can now pass almost $11,000,000 free of estate tax!

testified that the debtor intended to transfer the properties to avoid potential creditors.

The court held that the transfers were fraudulent because (1) the transfers were to an "insider," (2) the debtor was still in possession or control of the properties after the transfer, (3) the debtor was left with no substantial assets, (4) there was no consideration in exchange for the transfers, and (5) the debtor was insolvent after the transfer.

Note: In cases where the debtor has not filed bankruptcy, the creditor is the party who files a claim against the debtor under the GUFTA. In bankruptcy cases, the court appoints a trustee, who files a claim in bankruptcy court under the fraudulent transfers section of the United States Code at 11 U.S.C. § 548.

---

2. Fraudulent-transfer cases where the debtor filed bankruptcy.

a. Case in bankruptcy court; debtor in personal-injury suit makes transfer before trial (2013). The debtor, who was married, purchased property and put the property in his name; his spouse was not on the deed. The debtor was in an accident and sued by the injured party, whom the debtor knew had serious injuries and had missed a lot of work due to them. Before the trial began, the debtor transferred 50 percent of his residential property to his wife. The debtor claimed that his wife had helped pay for the property over the years of their marriage and that it was merely a mistake that the property had been put 100 percent in his name. Thus, by transferring 50 percent to her, he was simply making a correction. A year later, a judgment for $1,050,000 was issued against the debtor and, shortly thereafter, the debtor filed bankruptcy. The trustee claimed the transfer by the debtor to his spouse was a fraudulent transfer.

The court held that the transfer was fraudulent because (1) the wife never worked and barely contributed monetarily, (2) the transfer was made to an insider, and (3) the debtor still retained complete control of the property after the transfer.

b. Case in bankruptcy court; debtor corporation tries to avoid claim with transfer of valuable rugs to its main shareholder and sole officer (2013). The trustee sought to avoid a transfer of rugs from a corporation (debtor) to its main shareholder and sole officer. The debtor, a rug retailer, claimed that the transfer of rugs, worth more than $3 million, was to pay back the shareholder for a loan.

The court held that the transfer was fraudulent because (1) the transfer was made to an "insider," (2) adequate consideration was not given in exchange for the transfer, and (3) the debtor was insolvent at the time of the transfer.

c. Case in bankruptcy court; debtor transferred all his assets to a trust for his wife, but the debtor retained control of the transferred assets (2014). The trustee claimed that the debtor made fraudulent transfers to his wife and other entities for no consideration. The debtor had no assets of his own, no bank account, and received no salary from his work. Everything was placed in an irrevocable trust account in his wife's name.

The court held that since the debtor transferred all his assets to his wife, yet retained control over his wife's trust, the money transferred into the trust was considered a fraudulent conveyance to avoid his creditors.

Hudson's Tip: If you set up a trust, transfer property, or enter into a business arrangement and you expect creditors to respect it ... then you **must treat the trust, transfer, or business arrangement as bona fide.**

For example, no one works for free, yet the debtor in the above case took no salary. Also, when property is transferred in a bona fide transaction, the person who makes the transfer does not and should not remain in control of the property. When property is transferred and the person who transfers the property wants to use it, rent must be paid just like rent would be paid by a third party who wants to use the property. And a smart person realizes that paying rent removes more assets from the reach of creditors.

CHAPTER 5 RECAP:

1. If someone has a claim against you, and you transfer assets out of your name to someone close to you, and you do not receive reasonable value for the assets that you transfer, the "fraudulent transfer" laws in the Georgia code and in the federal bankruptcy code may enable that person to have the transfer voided and seize the transferred assets.

2. A "claim" can be a fixed and certain debt, such as a loan balance. A "claim" can also be uncertain and not yet fixed—for example, if you are at fault in an automobile accident, the person you injured has a "claim" against you for purposes of the fraudulent transfer laws, even though they have not yet filed or threatened to file a lawsuit against you.

3. With comprehensive asset-protection planning, there will be no need to fraudulently transfer any assets. You will be prepared ahead of time to deal with these types of creditors. Planning ahead is the best strategy for keeping your hard-earned assets safe.

C H A P T E R   6

USE OF TRUSTS IN ASSET-PROTECTION PLANNING FOR GEORGIA RESIDENTS

Trusts are used in two situations to protect a person's assets: The first situation involves a person who is fortunate enough to receive an inheritance or gift from someone, such as a parent, and the person who left the inheritance, made the gift, or set up a trust for the recipient. The person whom the trust is intended to benefit is called the "beneficiary" of the trust. This is a common fact pattern and this is how many trusts are formed. In the first situation, we will examine what happens when someone files a lawsuit against the beneficiary of the trust and the person who filed the lawsuit wants the beneficiary's interest (money) in the trust to satisfy the creditor's claim.

In the second situation, a person who wishes to protect his assets decides to create a trust and transfer some or all of his assets to the trust. The person who creates the trust is called the "settlor" of the trust. Typically, the trust that the settlor creates benefits someone other than the settlor. The idea here is that when someone files a lawsuit against the settlor, he can tell the person who filed the lawsuit that the assets in the trust are not his assets and the lawsuit has no impact on those assets. In the second situation, we will examine whether the settlor can keep the assets that he transferred to his trust out of the reach of his creditors.

This chapter addresses the following two situations:

1. Claims of creditors against a beneficiary of a trust set up by someone other than the beneficiary

2. Claims of creditors against the person who set up and transferred property or money to the trust

The basics. A *trust* is an arrangement that a person, called the "settlor" or "grantor," creates. Typically, the settlor transfers property or money to another person called the "trustee," who is required to hold and manage the transferred property in accordance with a written set of instructions that the settlor gives to the trustee. The written set of instructions is called the "trust agreement." The last person involved in a trust is the "beneficiary." The trustee holds and manages the trust property for the beneficiary.

Probably the most common trust arrangement involves a parent (the settlor), a child (the beneficiary), and another person (the trustee). The parent prepares the written set of instructions (the trust agreement). The parent selects a trustee (most often a relative or bank), and the trustee agrees to act and follow the terms of the trust agreement. Some of the parent's property or money is transferred to the trustee, and the trustee holds and manages the trust property or money for the beneficiary.

What a beneficiary is entitled to receive from a trust depends on the instructions in the trust agreement, and there are generally three types of beneficial interests.

1. The first type is where the beneficiary must be paid a fixed amount of money. For example, a trust agreement could provide that the beneficiary is entitled to all the income of the trust each year. Or, the trust agreement might provide that the beneficiary is entitled to $10,000 each year.

2. The second type of beneficial interest is where the beneficiary must receive an amount of money for specified needs. For example, the trustee must pay the amounts that are necessary to meet the beneficiary's educational and medical needs. Or, the trustee must pay for the beneficiary's support and living expenses (e.g., rent, auto, gas, or housing).

3. The third type is where the amount that the beneficiary receives is left up to the discretion of the trustee. The beneficiary may receive *nothing* in a given year! The trustee has the discretion to pay an amount—including $0—that the trustee determines to be in the "best interests" of the beneficiary. This type of trust is appropriately called a "discretionary trust."

1. Creditor tries to satisfy his claims against a beneficiary with assets that are in a trust.

When a beneficiary of a trust owes money to a creditor, the creditor is able to get whatever the beneficiary is entitled to receive from the trust in order to satisfy the claim. Accordingly, a trust agreement can be drafted to limit what a beneficiary is entitled to receive from a trust in order to minimize—or eliminate—the amount that the beneficiary's creditors can get from the trust. However, the creditors of the world, and certainly the creditors in Georgia, have been able to get some laws passed that protect, in certain situations, the creditors of trust beneficiaries. The two main ways to draft a trust in order to limit the rights of creditors against a trust beneficiary in Georgia are (a) use of a spendthrift clause and (b) use of a discretionary trust.

We will use the following fact pattern to illustrate the laws that determine whether a creditor can get a beneficiary's trust assets:

> A father creates a trust for the benefit of his son, who is forty-two years old, married with two children, and a partner with two other people in a real estate development business in Alpharetta, Georgia. The father believes that his son is responsible, but is concerned that his son's marriage is unstable and could end in divorce, like the father's first marriage. Further, the father is concerned about the ability of the son and his two business partners to repay a $2,500,000 bank loan for which the three partners signed jointly and for which each of the three partners is personally liable.

a. Use of "spendthrift clause" in a trust agreement to block creditors. A "spendthrift clause" is a special provision that can be included in a trust agreement. A typical spendthrift clause provides that (1) the beneficiary cannot give away his beneficial interest, (2) the beneficiary cannot pledge his beneficial interest as collateral for a loan, and (3) the beneficiary's creditors cannot seize his beneficial interest in the trust to satisfy debts that the beneficiary incurs.

> **Here is an example of a typical spendthrift clause:**
>
> The income and/or corpus from the trust for the beneficiary shall not be transferred, assigned, or conveyed by the beneficiary, and shall not be subject to the claims of any creditors of the beneficiary, and the trustee shall continue to manage and distribute such income and corpus for the support, maintenance, and welfare of such beneficiary, directly to or for the benefit of such beneficiary, notwithstanding any transfer, assignment, or conveyance, and notwithstanding any action by creditors.

Georgia trust law, which was revised in 2010, provides that spendthrift clauses are valid with respect to voluntary assignments by the beneficiary and, subject to special rules or modifications, involuntary assignments by creditors of the beneficiary. A voluntary assignment includes a gift by the beneficiary of his beneficial interest or pledging the beneficial interest as collateral on a loan. An involuntary assignment means that a creditor of a beneficiary is trying to take the trust property in order to satisfy a debt or obligation that the beneficiary has to the creditor. Examples of an involuntary assignment include (1) the beneficiary gets divorced, is ordered by the court to pay alimony to his ex-spouse, and beneficiary claims that he does not have enough money to pay his ex-spouse, so the ex-spouse tries to get the alimony paid from the trust; and, (2) the beneficiary and his partners fail to pay their bank loan, so the bank tries to get money from the beneficiary's trust.

In order for a spendthrift clause to be valid in Georgia, it must restrict both voluntary and involuntary assignments. So, you cannot have a spendthrift clause that restricts creditors of the beneficiary from trying to reach the trust assets (involuntary assignment), while allowing the beneficiary to assign (transfer) trust property (voluntary assignment).

> **Note:** Spendthrift clauses are important because without one, the beneficiary's creditors stand in the place of the beneficiary and are entitled to the benefits of the trust to satisfy the creditor's claim.

In Georgia, certain creditors of a beneficiary can reach the trust assets even when the trust has a spendthrift clause. The following claims against a beneficiary's right to a current distribution are allowed to the extent the distribution would be subject to garnishment if the distribution were disposable earnings and the claim is for

a) alimony or child support;

b) taxes or governmental claims;

c) tort judgments;

d) judgments or orders for restitution as a result of a criminal conviction of the beneficiary; or

e) judgments for necessities.

Georgia garnishment law generally provides that a creditor can garnish or take 25 percent of a person's "disposable earnings" (if distributed from the trust), except in the case of alimony or child support, in which event the amount a creditor can garnish or take is 50 percent of the person's disposable earnings. To illustrate: If the trust for the son/beneficiary provides that the trustee must pay the son all the income earned on the trust every year, and the income for 2014 is $2,000, and the creditor of the beneficiary has a claim described in (b), (c), (d) or (e) above, then for 2014 the creditor would be entitled to up to 25 percent of the $2,000, and the beneficiary would be able to keep the remaining 75 percent. If the creditor is a former spouse and has a claim for alimony or child support, the ex-spouse is entitled to up to 50 percent of the $2,000 for 2014. If the creditor's judgment is not satisfied in 2014, the creditor continues to get the 25 percent or 50 percent in 2015, and every year thereafter until the judgment is satisfied.

Spendthrift clauses can protect a beneficiary from business creditors—but not from taxes, criminal acts, former spouses, child support, debts for necessities of life (rent, mortgage, food, clothing, medical, etc.) or torts. A *tort* involves either a negligent act (e.g., the beneficiary is at fault in an automobile accident) or an intentional act (e.g., the beneficiary gets mad and punches someone in the nose) that injures another person or his or her property. The biggest judgments that the beneficiary may have could be for a tort, child support, or alimony, so spendthrift clauses may not help much in Georgia. Some creditors have the unique ability to reach the beneficiary's interest despite a spendthrift trust (e.g., Internal Revenue Service, Georgia Department of Revenue, ex-spouse who is due alimony or child support) and also have special status under other laws. For example, Georgia law provides that the Internal Revenue Service, the Georgia Department of Revenue, and a spouse and minor children have claims superior to all other creditors of a decedent's estate.

In Georgia, it's valid to have a spendthrift provision that contains a clause—I call it the "poison pill" clause—that provides that the beneficiary's interest in the trust will terminate if the beneficiary tries to voluntarily assign—or the beneficiary's creditors attempt to reach—the beneficiary's interest. Because the poison-pill clause is draconian, it is seldom used. However, if the trust switches to another beneficiary, such as the beneficiary's children, then the poison-pill clause could be useful.

Not surprisingly, Georgia law provides that a spendthrift clause is effective in a "special-needs trust" that is designed in accordance with federal law. A special-needs trust is one that is established for the benefit of a disabled person. One objective of a special-needs trust is that the assets transferred to the trust and the income generated by trust assets shall not be counted as a resource of the beneficiary—so the disabled beneficiary will be eligible to receive governmental assistance, such as Medicaid and Supplemental Security Income.

Georgia also has a special rule regarding a beneficiary's transfer of property or money to a trust containing a spendthrift clause. In that event, the beneficiary's creditors can reach a proportionate amount of the trust property or money. So, if the beneficiary contributes 50 percent of the property in the trust, the beneficiary's creditors can reach 50 percent of the trust assets. If the beneficiary contributes 100 percent, the creditors of the beneficiary can reach 100 percent.

b. Discretionary trusts to block creditors. The example above provides that the trust agreement *required* the trustee to pay the beneficiary all of the income of the trust every year, and the income for 2014 was $2,000. In that example, the trustee had no discretion—the trust agreement mandated that the trustee *must* pay the income. If, instead, the trust agreement gave the trustee *discretion* to determine *if* and *when* the trust income and property would be paid to the beneficiary, the trust would be classified as a discretionary trust.

Georgia Code Section 53–12–81 provides, in part, that except for the proportion of trust that the beneficiary contributed to the trust, a beneficiary's creditor cannot compel the trustee to pay any amount that is payable only in the trustee's discretion. Now we are getting somewhere!

So, if the son anticipates receiving an inheritance from his parents, and he wants to protect the inheritance from his future creditors, he could ask his parents to write their wills so that his inheritance will pass into a discretionary trust for his benefit.

Georgia Code Section 53–12–81 even permits the beneficiary of a discretionary trust to be the trustee of the trust! However, there are risks and problems with

> *Hudson's Tip:* With a discretionary trust, a significant planning opportunity exists for Georgia residents who have a moderate- or high-risk assessment and who anticipate receiving an inheritance.

being the trustee *and* beneficiary of a discretionary trust. First, tax laws provide that the assets in the trust will be included in the beneficiary/trustee's estate for estate-tax purposes. Still, that might be less of a concern now than it was in the past, since the federal estate tax exemption is currently $5,490,000 per person and the exemption amount is indexed to increase. Second, Georgia Code Section 53–12–270 provides, in general, that a person who is a trustee and beneficiary of a trust cannot make discretionary distributions to himself, unless the trust agreement expressly waives the application of Section 53–12–270. Third, if there is another beneficiary of the trust, in addition to the beneficiary/trustee, the beneficiary/trustee would likely be in a conflict of interest since the trustee would have the choice (conflict) of making distributions to himself and the other beneficiary. Fourth, a contract creditor might claim that the beneficiary/trustee is binding and obligating the trust under a contract in his capacity as trustee, instead of his capacity as a beneficiary, in which case the contract creditor could reach the trust assets. The beneficiary/trustee will need to sign contracts and agreements "As trustee" and make sure that the assets of the trust remain segregated and separate from his personal assets to avoid this type of claim from a creditor.

Instead of the beneficiary being the trustee of the discretionary trust, it would probably be better to have a trusted friend, sibling, or other relative be the trustee—or at least be a cotrustee with the trustee/beneficiary.

Another issue with a discretionary trust is that, well, the trustee has *discretion*. To be certain that the trust is not subject to creditor claims, the trust agreement should be drafted in such a way that the trustee has *total discretion*. However, leaving absolute discretion to another person could be dangerous, unless all parties have a high degree of confidence and trust (no pun intended) in the person being considered to serve as the trustee. Also, most trusts name a successor or back-up trustee in case the desired trustee can no longer perform the duties, so the same level of confidence is needed for the back-up trustee. Being the trustee of a discretionary trust can be, in certain situations, quite difficult, because the trustee has to be in closer communication with the beneficiary and must decide whether or not the beneficiary will receive money. It is much easier to serve as the trustee of a trust that provides specific guidance to the trustee—such as paying all the income to the beneficiary each year.

2. Claims of a creditor against the settlor of a trust.

a. The general rule for Georgia residents: self-settled trusts do not work. Georgia law provides that a settlor cannot create a trust, transfer property to the trust, name him- or herself as a beneficiary of the trust, and prevent the settlor's creditors from reaching the assets of the trust. A trust created by a settlor for the settlor's benefit is referred to as *self-settled trust*.

As we saw in chapter 5, sometimes a person transfers assets to a trust for the benefit of another, such as his spouse. If the person is making a fraudulent transfer, the assets transferred to a trust—even a trust of which the settlor is not a beneficiary—can be subject to the claims of creditors of the settlor and can be seized by the creditors. However, if the transfer of assets to a trust for the benefit of another person is not a fraudulent transfer, then trust assets may be beyond the reach of the settlor's creditors. If the Georgia trust is a discretionary trust, the trust should also be beyond the reach of all creditors of the beneficiary!

b. States that permit self-settled trusts. There are currently sixteen states, including our neighbor Tennessee, that have enacted laws that allow a person to form a self-settled trust, and, if certain conditions are

States Permitting Self-Settled Trusts/DAPTs:

1. Nevada
2. South Dakota
3. Ohio
4. Tennessee
5. Alaska
6. Wyoming
7. Delaware
8. Missouri
9. New Hampshire
10. Hawaii
11. Rhode Island
12. Utah
13. Virginia
14. Mississippi
15. Oklahoma
16. West Virginia

met, the assets transferred to the self-settled trust will be free from many (but not all) claims of the settlor's creditors. A trust created under such a law is referred to as a domestic asset-protection trust, or DAPT for short. We refer to a state that has passed laws authorizing the creation of these trusts as a DAPT state. It appears that a resident of a DAPT state *may* receive some creditor-protection benefits from forming a self-settled trust in accordance with the state's statutes. However, most DAPT states permit claims of an ex-spouse and child-support claims, and most DAPT states require that at least one trustee be a resident or trust company of that particular state who did *not* contribute assets to the trust.

c. Can Georgia residents use DAPTs? Georgia is not a DAPT state, but legislation was proposed to make Georgia a DAPT state. It is not known if the legislation will be proposed again and if Georgia will ever allow DAPTs. In any case, the big question is this: Can a Georgia resident drive up to Tennessee (or any other DAPT state), establish a DAPT, transfer assets to the DAPT, and exempt the DAPT's assets from his creditors?

Georgia Code Section 53–12–5 permits the settlor of a trust to designate the law of a specified state or country to apply to the trust, unless the effect of the designation is contrary to the public policy of the jurisdiction having the most significant relationship to the matter at issue. So, Section 53–12–5 requires a determination of (1) which state law is designated in the trust agreement, (2) which state has the "most significant relationship to the matter," and (3) whether the effect of the designation is contrary to the laws of the state with the most significant relationship to the matter.

Two recent Georgia cases illustrating Section 53–12–5 are *In re Dorsey*, 497 B.R. 374, 384 (Bankr. N.D. Ga. 2013) and *Morris v.*

Morris, 326 Ga. App. 378, 381, 756 S.E.2d 616, 619 (2014), cert. denied (June 16, 2014).

In the *Dorsey* case, a spendthrift trust was set up by a parent—residing in Maryland—for the benefit of a child. The trust was administered in Maryland and the trust agreement provided that Maryland law would apply. The beneficiary of the trust—who lived in Georgia—filed bankruptcy in Georgia. The beneficiary claimed that the spendthrift trust was not part of his bankruptcy estate. The court did not give an analysis of whether Georgia or Maryland had the most significant relationship, but held that since both Maryland and Georgia recognize the general validity of spendthrift trusts, there was no reason (public policy or otherwise) *not* to apply Maryland law. Presumably the facts that the settlor of the trust was a Maryland resident and the trust was administered in Maryland by a Maryland trustee made Maryland the state with the most significant relationship, even though the beneficiary lived in Georgia and filed bankruptcy in Georgia.

In the *Morris* case, a settlor created a trust when he was a resident of Georgia, another Georgia resident was the trustee, and the trust agreement provided that Georgia law would apply. The trust agreement provided that, upon the settlor's death, the trust would be paid to his daughter if she survived him. After setting up the trust, the settlor moved to North Carolina and lived there for five years. During the entire existence of the trust, it was held and administered in Georgia. The settlor's daughter traveled from her home in Georgia to visit the settlor at his North Carolina home—and during that visit, the settlor killed his daughter and then killed himself. Under North Carolina law, a person who is murdered is deemed to survive the murderer. The daughter's estate argued that North Carolina law applied to the trust agreement, instead of Georgia law, and since the daughter is deemed to have survived the settlor under North Carolina law, her estate should get the trust money. Georgia did not have a law similar to North Carolina's murder-survivor law. Under Georgia law, the trust money would go to the *contingent beneficiaries* (people designated to receive the trust money if the daughter did not survive the settlor) named in the trust agreement. The court held that Georgia had the most significant relationship to the matter at issue because

- the trust was executed in Georgia, and at that time all parties to the trust resided in Georgia with the trust;

- the trust was always held and administered by the Georgia trustee in Georgia; and lastly,

- the court held that since Georgia did not have a law similar to North Carolina's murderer-survivor law, so there was no public-policy reason not to apply Georgia law.

In the *Dorsey* and *Morris* cases, Georgia courts held that the state law that was designated in the trust agreement to be the state with the most significant relationship to the matter, and public policy of the state did not prohibit the effect of the designated state law.

So how would a Georgia court apply Section 53–12–5 to a situation where a creditor sues a Georgia resident who creates a trust in Tennessee, or another DAPT state, and the trust is held and administered in the DAPT state? Add the fact that at least one trustee resides in the DAPT state. Georgia courts have not ruled on this situation yet. However, if a 2013 bankruptcy court case in Washington state—the *Huber* case—can be used as a guide, it appears that a Georgia court will hold that Georgia has the most significant contacts, and since Georgia prohibits self-settled trusts, Georgia law will likely allow the creditor to reach the trust assets.

CASE STUDY: DAPT CHOICE OF LAW ISSUES

Waldron v. Huber (In re Huber),
493 B.R. 798 (2013)

- Mr. Huber was a residential-home developer with more than forty years of experience.

- In 2008, through his company (UWD), he tried to raise $55 million, but was unsuccessful due to the real estate market turmoil.

- Mr. Huber was in a partnership on many projects with Mr. Terhune. Huber pressured Terhune to pay monies that he believed Terhune owed him. Terhune threatened to set up his own spendthrift trust, and Huber's attorney made it clear to Terhune that the creation of such a trust would be fraudulent as to Huber—as Huber considered himself a creditor of Terhune.

- Huber and several of his entities were sued by financial institutions for failure to pay loans.

- Huber's son sent an e-mail to his father's attorney stating that "my father has some assets that he would like to protect and shield."

- Huber transferred $10,000 and his ownership interest in twenty-five entities to an Alaska LLC, which was 99 percent owned by a self-settled Alaska trust and 1 percent owned by Huber's son. Alaska is a DAPT state, and the trust provided that Alaska law governed the trust.

- The three trustees of the trust were an Alaska trust company and a son and daughter of Mr. Huber. Both the son and daughter lived in Washington.

- The beneficiaries of the trust were Huber and his children, all of whom lived in Washington.

- Mr. Huber filed bankruptcy, and the bankruptcy trustee argued that the trust should be invalidated under Washington law—because Washington law prohibits self-settled trusts.

- Federal bankruptcy law provides that the state law designated by the settlor to govern the trust shall be respected *if* the state has a substantial relation to the trust and the application of its law does not violate a strong public policy of the state with which the trust has its most significant relations. (Federal bankruptcy law is *very similar* to Georgia Code Section 53–12–5.)

- Next, the court held that a state has a substantial relation to the trust, if at the time the trust is created, (a) the trustee or settlor is domiciled in the state, (b) the assets are located in the state, and (c) the beneficiaries are domiciled in the state.

- The court held that since (a) the settlor was domiciled in Washington; (b) two of the three trustees were domiciled in Washington; (c) all the beneficiaries were domiciled in Washington; and (d) all the trust assets, except for a $10,000 certificate of deposit, were located in Washington; the state with a substantial relation to the trust was—not Alaska.

- The court noted that Washington has a policy and law against self-settled trusts, and that a debtor should not be able to escape the claims of his creditors by utilizing a spendthrift trust.

- The court held that Washington law applied, and thus Mr. Huber's transfers were void under Washington's law that prohibited the use of self-settled trusts for creditor protection.

- The court further held that the transfers were fraudulent transfers because of the existence of five badges of fraud (discussed in chapter 5).

Therefore, it is highly likely that a Georgia court would hold that Georgia law, *not* the designated law of a DAPT state, would apply to a DAPT, with the result that Georgia's public policy of a debtor not being able to escape the claims of his creditors by utilizing a spendthrift trust would control and give the creditor access to the assets.

There are two other reasons that Georgia residents seeking to benefit from a DAPT will likely fail. The first reason is the *Full Faith and Credit* clause of the United States Constitution, which provides: "Full faith and credit shall be given in each State to the public acts, records and judicial proceedings of every other state." The effect of the clause is that once a creditor obtains a judgment against a debtor in one state—such as Georgia—against a person or business, the creditor can take his judgment to another state—such as Tennessee— and Tennessee courts must enforce the Georgia judgment against the debtor or his property in Tennessee. If this were not the case, a debtor could escape a judgment in one state by simply moving to a different one. The United States Constitution, which trumps state laws, provides that once a creditor gets a judgment against a debtor in one state, the creditor can take his judgment to other states where the debtor has property.

Because DAPTs are relatively new, there are no reported cases where the Full Faith and Credit clause has been used against a DAPT. However, the 2012 bankruptcy court case of *In re Inman* involves the application of the Full Faith and Credit Clause. In that case, a Florida creditor got a judgment against a Florida debtor, and the Florida creditor asked a court in Colorado to apply the Florida judgment to the debtor's Colorado property. The court ruled that the Full Faith and Credit Clause permitted the creditor to seize the debtor's property in Colorado. A more detailed discussion of the *Inman* case appears in chapter 7.

The third reason that Georgia residents may have difficulty using a DAPT concerns changes to the bankruptcy code, which create a new ten-year limitations period for transfers to self-settled trusts that are meant to hinder, delay, or defraud creditors. So, for persons who may contemplate filing bankruptcy in the future, the creation of and transfers to a DAPT will likely be scrutinized for the ten-year period before filing bankruptcy. The 2011 case of *In re Mortensen* illustrates the ten-year lookback rule for a self-settled trust.

CASE STUDY: BANKRUPTCY: TEN-YEAR STATUTE OF LIMITATIONS

In re Mortensen, US Bankruptcy Court, District of Alaska (2011)

- Thomas Mortensen was involved in a nasty divorce that he claimed "saddled him with debt" and caused him financial trouble.

- Mortensen, an Alaska resident, created a DAPT in Alaska in February 2005.

- He deeded real property to his DAPT on the date of formation.

- An express purpose of the DAPT was "to maximize the protection of the trust estate or estates from creditors' claims of the grantor or any beneficiary."

- Mortensen filed for chapter 7 bankruptcy relief in August 2009—four years and five months after he created the DAPT and transferred real estate to his DAPT.

- The bankruptcy trustee moved to have the real property conveyance voided because it was a fraudulent transfer under the Federal Bankruptcy Act.

- It was determined that Mortensen was insolvent at the time the DAPT was created.

- In Alaska, fraudulent transfers have a four-year "lookback" or statute of limitations period where they can be voided. Mr. Mortensen was relying on this law when he filed for bankruptcy just five months after the four-year lookback period expired.

- However, the recently enacted Bankruptcy Abuse Protection and Consumer Protection Act (BAPCPA) allows a ten-year lookback period for transfers made to a self-settled trust.

- The court applied the federal bankruptcy law and, therefore, the transfer of the real property to the DAPT was voided by the court and deemed a fraudulent transfer.

   d. Countries that permit self-settled trust. There are a number of island nations and small countries (Nevis, the Bahamas, Isle of Mann, Belize, Cayman Islands, and Cook Islands, to name a few) that have enacted laws that authorize self-settled trusts and also have fraudulent-transfer laws that are favorable to people trying to protect their assets from creditors. It is reported that the architects of some of these foreign laws are American lawyers who specialize in debtor/creditor laws. Most of these countries also impose a requirement that a creditor seeking to reach the assets of a debtor or customer's trust must post an expensive bond prior to proceeding with a lawsuit and, generally, try to make the hunt for assets difficult.

   Perhaps the most significant claim or feature of the foreign jurisdictions is that they do not have to obey United States courts and that there is no Full Faith and Credit Clause that applies to them. However, there are a couple of issues that can arise. First, if the debtor continues to live in and be a citizen of the United States, then the debtor *is* subject to the jurisdiction and orders of US courts. Second, if the money transferred to a foreign jurisdiction returns to the United States, the debtor has to pay the

> **Hudson's Tip:** Creating offshore trusts can be very time-consuming and expensive and takes a high level of compliance and sophistication. However, once an offshore account is established, it can be very effective.

creditor. What happened in the United States (the debtor's debts and the lawsuits) did not disappear.

Many promoters of offshore trusts are either not lawyers or are lawyers who are licensed to practice law in neither Georgia nor the foreign country. And how can such persons give advice to a Georgia resident on *any* legal matter, much less on use of an offshore trust?

e. Does a Georgia resident really need a self-settled trust? I hear people say that the reason they want a self-settled trust is because they are afraid of losing control of, or access to, the assets transferred to the trust. But is that what happens when a person transfers assets to a trust where he or she is neither the beneficiary nor the trustee? If you set up a discretionary trust, one purpose of which is to pay for your children's college education, and your sibling or parent is the trustee of the trust ... have you lost those assets? No. The assets have merely been placed into a protected environment and will be invested and used for your children's college education.

You are simply moving assets that you intend to use for a family member and that are subject to potential creditor claims into a trust that will benefit the family member, but will not be subject to creditor claims. I often characterize this as "moving money from a pocket of your pants that is open to another pocket that has a zipper." The money is still in your pants!

One objection I hear to moving unprotected assets in a person's name to a protected trust for that person's spouse is: **"What if I put some of my assets in a trust for the benefit of my spouse and we get divorced?"** Answer: The trust agreement can include a provision that your spouse will automatically lose beneficiary status if you and him or her stops living together as husband and wife. Note that for the provision to be activated and your spouse removed as a beneficiary does not require an order from the court to the effect that you and your spouse are divorced, since most people who get a divorce stop living together long before a court issues a final decree of divorce.

Another objection is: **"I must be in control of my money and, in the future, I might need those assets that I transferred to the trust."** If you think that the beneficiary of the trust would consider making a loan or gift to you, then you might be okay. Also, if you think that the trustee of the trust would make a loan to you, you might be okay. However, you cannot have an agreement, implicit or otherwise, for the trustee or beneficiary to make trust funds available to you, and any loan to you would need to be on the same terms that you would get from a bank—that is, a commercial interest rate, adequate security, regular payments of principal and interest, and a fixed and definite term or time for the loan to be repaid.

A recommended course of action is to set up the trust for the benefit of family members and start transferring small amounts of money or assets to the trust over a period of years. This way, you can see if the arrangement works for everyone. If you are not comfortable continuing to transfer money to the trust, you simply stop. If everything seems to be working out, you can continue to transfer assets to the trust. If all is done properly, you will have created a pool of assets that are protected from your future creditors and the creditors of the beneficiaries, your family members.

Not everyone has a family situation that allows for the transfer of assets to a trust. If you do not have such a situation, do not despair … there are other ways to protect your assets.

CHAPTER 6 RECAP:

- For a "spendthrift clause" in a trust agreement to be valid in Georgia, the clause must prohibit (1) the beneficiary from transferring or assigning his interest in the trust; *and* (2) creditors of the beneficiary from reaching the beneficiary's interest in the trust.

- With respect to creditor claims against a beneficiary of a trust:

  - Notwithstanding a valid "spendthrift clause," certain creditor claims are permitted against a beneficiary's right to mandatory trust distributions. These special creditors can generally take up to 25 percent of the mandatory distribution. The IRS and the Georgia Department of Revenue are examples of these special creditors. A former spouse with an alimony or child-support claim is also a special creditor, but an ex-spouse can take up to 50 percent of the mandatory distribution.

  - Under Georgia law, a "discretionary trust" can prevent any creditor from reaching a beneficiary's interest, since there are no mandatory distributions to the beneficiary.

- A great planning opportunity exists for persons who have creditor concerns and are likely to inherit valuable assets from their parents. The parents can create a discretionary trust in a will, instead of leaving the inheritance outright.

- Under Georgia law, a Georgia resident cannot transfer his or her assets to a self-settled trust (a trust of which the settlor is also the beneficiary) for purposes of placing the trust assets beyond the reach of his creditors. It is unlikely that the Georgia resident will be able to use a DAPT created in another state, but there is a possibility that a DAPT set up in a neighboring state, like Tennessee, would work for a resident of Tennessee.

- Assuming no "fraudulent transfers" are made, a Georgia resident should be able to place assets beyond the reach of his or her creditors and the creditors of a beneficiary/family member by transferring such assets to a properly-structured discretionary trust.

C H A P T E R   7

WHAT IS THE DEAL WITH TENNESSEE, NEVADA, DELAWARE, AND FLORIDA LLCs—AND DO GEORGIA RESIDENTS NEED THESE ENTITIES?

Limited liability companies (LLCs) are special entities, which, in terms of legal history, are relatively new. The first state to enact an LLC statute was Wyoming, in 1977. However, it was not until 1988 (the year I started practicing law), when the Internal Revenue Service issued Revenue Ruling 88–76 and "blessed" the favorable income tax and limited liability features of LLCs, that LLCs really took off. Georgia passed its LLC Act in 1993 and the first Georgia LLC was formed in 1994.

An LLC enjoys the favorable income tax rules of partnerships, has more flexibility than "S" corporations, and affords the LLC owners liability protection from the LLC's debts and liabilities in a way similar to the manner in which a corporation shields its shareholders from liabilities of their corporation. The LLC is essentially part partnership and part corporation—the best of both worlds.

Today, LLCs are now formed more frequently than corporations in Georgia. The LLC is now the "king" of entities, and it is unlikely that corporations will ever take back the title.

The owners of a corporation are called shareholders. The shareholders of a corporation own shares in the corporation. Each share contains both economic rights (for example, the right to dividends) and governance rights (for example, the right to vote).

The owners of an LLC are called members. The economic and governance rights can be separated in LLCs. In Georgia, a "limited liability company interest" means a member's share of the profits and losses of an LLC and a member's right to receive distributions—the economic rights.

The management of an LLC is vested in either the members or the manager(s). If management is vested in the members, then the members have the right to vote on management matters. Most LLCs have an "operating agreement" that details (1) whether management of the LLC is vested in the members or managers; (2) what happens to a member's interest when the member dies or becomes disabled; (3) what happens to a member's interest if the member files bankruptcy; (4) how much money each member is required to invest in the LLC; and (5) the ownership percentage of each member.

LLCs have adopted the partnership principle of "pick your partner." Partnerships and LLCs are relationships of trust between chosen partners, and the theory is that no one should be required to go into business with persons who are not of his or her choosing.

The concepts of (a) separate economic and management interests in LLCs and (b) "picking your partner" are important in understanding the rights, or perhaps more accurately the limitations, that a judgment creditor has when dealing with a debtor who is a member of an LLC. For example, the pick-your-partner concept has been used as the basis for laws and contract provisions that prohibit a creditor of an LLC member from seizing the member's interest in the LLC and allowing the creditor to become a new member of the LLC—the other members of the LLC did not pick the creditor to be a member of the LLC, so the creditor must stay out.

IF A GEORGIA RESIDENT IS A MEMBER OF A GEORGIA LLC AND HAS NOT FILED BANKRUPTCY, WHAT CAN A JUDGMENT CREDITOR DO WITH THE MEMBER'S LLC INTEREST?

A judgment creditor is a creditor who has filed a lawsuit against someone, won the lawsuit, and been awarded a judgment by the court—that is, a creditor with a judgment. The judgment issued by the court declares that the creditor is entitled to a certain dollar amount from the person he or she sued, a.k.a. the debtor. Georgia Code Section 14–11–504 details what a judgment creditor can do when the debtor is a member of an LLC. One thing a judgment creditor can do is to ask the court to issue a "charging order" against the member's "limited liability company interest" (the economic interest). A charging order is essentially a lien against the member's LLC interest, which stays in place until the judgment is satisfied. A charging order only gives the judgment creditor the right to receive money that otherwise would have been paid to the member of the LLC who owes money to the judgment creditor.

Charging Order: A court document that directs the manager(s) of an LLC to divert distributions that would otherwise go to the debtor-member to the judgment creditor, to the extent of the creditor's unpaid judgment plus interest. A judgment creditor must file a petition and ask a judge to issue a charging order.

Georgia law respects the pick-your-partner principle by prohibiting a judgment creditor from obtaining control or management rights in the LLC. Section 14–11–504(b) of the Georgia Code provides that when a creditor receives a judgment against an LLC member, the creditor may not interfere in the management of the LLC or take certain other actions that would be disruptive to the company's business. The creditor cannot order the LLC to make distributions just because the creditor has a charging order. The creditor is entitled to get the money that the member would otherwise receive, nothing else.

There are some states, like Tennessee, Delaware, and Nevada, that limit the remedy of a judgment creditor against a person who is a member in an LLC to a charging order. Georgia does not limit the remedies available to a judgment creditor against a member in an LLC to a charging order, but Georgia does prohibit the remedies of interference in the LLC management, of dissolution of the LLC, and of a court-ordered foreclosure sale of the member's LLC interest. Georgia Code Section 14–11–504 provides that charging orders

> "shall not be deemed exclusive of other remedies which may exist, including without limitation, the right of a judgment creditor to reach the limited liability company

interest of the member by process of garnishment served on the LLC; provided that, except as otherwise provided in the articles of organization or a written operating agreement, a judgment creditor shall have no right under this chapter or any other state law to interfere with the management or force dissolution of a limited liability company or to seek an order of the court requiring a foreclosure sale of the limited liability company interest."

So, unless a Georgia LLC's articles of organization or written operating agreement permit, a judgment creditor can neither foreclose on a member's LLC interest nor force dissolution of the LLC.

It is important to note that Georgia Code Section 14–11–504 deals only with "judgment creditors," not secured creditors. A secured creditor is a person who has asked a member of an LLC to pledge the member's LLC interest as collateral for a debt or other obligation and received a security interest in the member's LLC interest from the LLC member. For example, in *Hopson v. Bank of North Georgia (2002)*, after a borrower defaulted on a loan, the bank sought to foreclose its security interest in the guarantor's LLC interest. As a condition to receiving the loan, Mr. Hopson signed a security agreement that assigned all of his right, title, and interest as a member of an LLC to the bank. When the bank foreclosed on the loan, Hopson claimed that Georgia Code Section 14–11–504 prohibited the bank from taking his LLC interest. The court pointed out that Section 14–11–504 only deals with judgment creditors—not secured creditors—and, thus, the bank was entitled to the economic interest of the LLC interest.

IS THERE A DIFFERENT RESULT IF THE
LLC ONLY HAS ONE MEMBER?

One important way that LLCs differ from partnerships is that an LLC can have only one member, while a partnership must have two or more partners. While many LLCs have two or more members, there may be just as many LLCs that have only one member. An LLC that only has one member is called a *single-member LLC*, or "SMLLC" for short. An LLC that has more than one member is referred to as *multiple-member LLC*, or "MMLLC."

With a SMLLC, it does not seem that the pick-your-partner rationale for keeping creditors out of the LLC would apply. However, Georgia Code Section 14–11–504, which forbids a judgment creditor from certain remedies—such as foreclosing on a membership interest—makes no distinction when a judgment creditor has a judgment against either an SMLLC or an MMLLC.

To date, there is no reported case in Georgia involving a judgment creditor who argued that Section 14–11–504 should not limit a judgment creditor when the LLC only has one member, but it seems that such an argument by a judgment creditor would be logical. However, in a 2010 case decided by the Florida Supreme Court, *Olmstead v. Federal Trade Commission*, 44 So. 3d 76 (Florida 2010), a judgment creditor sought to seize the interest of a member who owned 100 percent of an LLC. Florida had a statute, like Georgia, that provided that a judgment creditor of an LLC member was entitled to a charging order. The Florida Supreme Court held that the judgment creditor had remedies in addition to the charging order, and since the member of the SMLLC could transfer his LLC interest without restriction, the creditor was entitled to seize the membership interest.

Could a Georgia court reach the same conclusion? Maybe—but one difference between the Georgia and Florida statutes is that Georgia's statute expressly provides that a judgment creditor cannot "seek an order of the court requiring a foreclosure sale of the limited liability company interest"—and Florida's statute did not prohibit a creditor from seeking a foreclosure sale. After the *Olmstead* case, Florida amended its statute to expressly provide that the *exclusive* remedy of a judgment creditor against a member of an MMLLC is a charging order, but that under certain circumstances a judgment creditor can foreclose on the interest of a member in an SMLLC.

If possible, it is advisable for a Georgia LLC to have at least two members. For example, instead of a husband being the sole member of an LLC, his wife could own a meaningful percentage of the LLC, say 50 percent. However, a smaller percentage, such as 5 percent might also work.

IF A GEORGIA RESIDENT FILES BANKRUPTCY AND IS A MEMBER OF A GEORGIA LLC, THE RULES ABOUT CREDITORS REACHING THE MEMBER'S LLC INTEREST CHANGE SUBSTANTIALLY.

First, a little background on bankruptcy. Bankruptcy is a federal program. Federal laws govern the bankruptcy process, and federal courts known as "bankruptcy courts" handle bankruptcy cases. In Georgia, there are three bankruptcy courts, each with several judges: the Southern District (which has courts in Savannah, Augusta, Brunswick, Statesboro, Waycross, and Dublin), the Middle District (which has courts in Albany, Athens, Columbus, Thomasville, and Macon), and the Northern District (which has courts in Newnan, Atlanta, Rome, and Gainesville).

When a person files for bankruptcy, he or she becomes known as the "debtor." The debtor is required to file a list of assets and liabilities, including the names and addresses of each of his or her creditors. The bankruptcy court appoints a person called a "bankruptcy trustee" to oversee and administer the debtor's bankruptcy case. The bankruptcy trustee is an impartial party who does not represent the debtor or any of his creditors. As is more fully discussed in chapter 8, bankruptcy law allows a debtor to keep some of his assets; those assets are referred to as "exempt assets." One duty of the bankruptcy trustee is to collect and sell the debtor's nonexempt assets.

Georgia LLC law and operating agreements versus federal bankruptcy law. Georgia Code Section 14–11–601.1(b)(4) provides that, subject to contrary provisions in an LLC's operating agreement, a person ceases to be a member of an LLC at the time the person files a voluntary bankruptcy petition. In addition, and as noted above, most LLC operating agreements provide that the bankruptcy of a member triggers the right of the LLC and of the remaining members to purchase the bankrupt member's LLC interest within a certain period of time. If that option is not exercised, most operating agreements provide that the bankruptcy trustee will become an "assignee" only, and the bankruptcy trustee will *not* become a member of the LLC with attendant voting rights and management rights *unless* the LLC and the other members agree to admit the bankruptcy trustee as a member. Remember, an "assignee" of an LLC interest only has the right to money distributed from the LLC that would have otherwise been paid to the debtor-member. An assignee does not have a right to vote or participate in the management of the LLC. Of course, the LLC and the other members do not want a bankruptcy trustee to become a member, because the bankruptcy trustee could become involved in the management of the LLC' s business and affairs.

Clauses in operating agreements (or partnership agreements) that are triggered by a member's bankruptcy filing—like a provision that requires the LLC and other members to give their consent to the bankruptcy trustee becoming a member—are called *ipso facto* clauses.[4] Guess what? Bankruptcy law provides that *ipso facto* clauses that prohibit a bankruptcy trustee from taking a debtor's membership interest in an LLC are *not binding* on a bankruptcy trustee. In addition, if Georgia law (or the law of any other state) has the effect of prohibiting a bankruptcy trustee from taking a debtor's membership interest in an LLC, the state law will not be binding on the bankruptcy trustee.[5]

> **NOTE:** As more fully explained in chapter 8, there are a number of laws in Georgia that have an impact on a creditor trying to reach a person's assets, but once the person files for federal bankruptcy protection, those Georgia laws are superseded and the bankruptcy laws apply. So there a set of laws for a person who files bankruptcy (called "inside bankruptcy") and a different set of laws for the same person who has not filed bankruptcy ("outside bankruptcy"). For example, Georgia law provides that for "outside bankruptcy," the cash value of a person's life insurance or annuity is exempt from creditor process. However, once that same person files bankruptcy and is "inside bankruptcy," only a few thousand dollars' worth of the life insurance cash value and the annuity are exempt from creditors.

---

4   *Ipso facto* is a Latin phrase that means "by the fact itself."

5   Section 541(c)(1) of the bankruptcy code provides that the member's interest in the LLC becomes property of the bankruptcy estate notwithstanding any provision in an agreement, transfer instrument, or applicable non-bankruptcy law (A) that restricts or conditions transfer of such interest by the debtor; or (B) that is conditioned on the insolvency or financial condition of the debtor, on the commencement of a case under this title, or on the appointment of or taking possession by a trustee in a case under this title or a custodian before such commencement, and that effects or gives an option to effect a forfeiture, modification, or termination of the debtor's interest in property.

If an LLC operating agreement is an "executory" contract, it may be possible to prevent a bankruptcy trustee from becoming a member of the LLC. In general, an executory contract is an agreement where each party to the contract owes significant duties to each other, like contributing substantial managerial services or advice or continually contributing cash or capital. To determine whether an operating agreement is an "executory" contract, bankruptcy courts look to see if there is "some material obligation" owing to the LLC by the member/debtor. If the operating agreement is executory, the bankruptcy trustee will *not* be permitted to undertake the duties of the debtor to the LLC.

There is an entire section of the bankruptcy code, Section 365, which deals with executory contracts. The overwhelming majority of bankruptcy courts that have addressed the issue of whether an operating agreement is executory have found them to be nonexecutory. Below are the only three bankruptcy court cases I have found (none of which is in Georgia) where the court held that an LLC operating agreement *was* executory, and therefore prevented a bankruptcy trustee from becoming a member of the LLC.

- *Matter of Daughtery Const., Inc.,* 188 B.R. 607 (Bankr. D. Ned. 1995).

- *In re Allentown Ambassadors, Inc.,* 361 B.R. 422 (Bankr. E.D. Pa. 2007).

- *In re DeLuca,* 194 B.R. 65 (Bankr. E. D. Va. 1996).

> **CAUTION:** If an LLC's operating agreement contains a provision that obligates the debtor-member to perform substantial, ongoing duties, but there is no history of the debtor-member performing the referenced duties, then a bankruptcy court may ignore the provisions.

In the Georgia bankruptcy case of *In re H & W Food Mart,* the court determined that an LLC's operating agreement was *not* executory and, therefore, the bankruptcy trustee was able to become a member of the LLC with the right to vote. In this case, the debtor was a 50 percent member.

CASE STUDY

In re H & W Food Mart, LLC
461 B.R. 904 (2011)

- Jeffrey Hunt and Dewey Welch were each 50 percent owners of a convenience store and gas station in Villa Rica, Georgia, and formed an LLC for their company in 2003.

- In 2008, Hunt filed for Chapter 7 bankruptcy relief. A trustee was appointed and the trustee attempted to take and liquidate Hunt's 50 percent ownership interest in order to repay Hunt's debtors.

- The LLC's operating agreement required the other member of the LLC, Welch, to consent to the bankruptcy trustee becoming a member. However, the court noted that if the operating agreement was not executory, then Welch's consent was not required and the bankruptcy trustee could become a member of the LLC.

- The court explained that if the operating agreement was an executory contract, then the trustee could not become an LLC member in Hunt's place, because Hunt would have outstanding obligations to the LLC.

- The court looked at the operating agreement to see if there were any material obligations owed to the LLC by Hunt. The court found that the operating agreement did not impose any obligation on Hunt to make cash contributions or act in a managerial capacity. Accordingly, the court held that (1) the operating agreement was not executory, (2) the provision of the operating agreement that required the consent of the other member was not effective in bankruptcy, and (3) the bankruptcy trustee was entitled to become a member of the LLC.

INSIDE OF BANKRUPTCY, IS THERE A DIFFERENT RESULT IF THE LLC ONLY HAS ONE MEMBER?

Yes. Bankruptcy courts have held that where the member of an SMLLC files for bankruptcy relief, the bankruptcy trustee succeeds to all of the debtor's rights, including the right to control the LLC. There is no need to determine if there is an executory operating agreement or look at state law. The recent case of *In re Cleveland* (US District Court, District of Nevada, 2014), which held that the bankruptcy trustee automatically takes over the member's interest in an SMLLC, is interesting for a couple of reasons. First, many people tout Nevada as having laws favoring debtors and tout the Nevada LLC as the next panacea, because Nevada has a law that provides that the exclusive remedy of a judgment creditor of a member of an LLC is a charging order. The court in *In re Cleveland* reminded everyone that federal bankruptcy law, not state law, *controls the administration of property interests that are part of the bankruptcy estate.* The other interesting point of the *In re Cleveland* case is that the debtor argued that the bankruptcy trustee could not own or manage the LLC because the LLC provided specific professional or personal services. The court agreed that the bankruptcy trustee was not capable of providing those unique personal services, but the bankruptcy trustee could still liquidate the assets of the SMLLC.

> **Important Difference between Georgia Entities:** The main entities in Georgia are the corporation, the LLC, the limited liability partnerships (LLP), the limited partnership (LP), the limited liability limited partnership (LLLP), and the general partnership (GP). Under the Georgia statutes concerning LLCs, LLPs, and GPs, the foreclosure of a member-partner's interest is expressly forbidden, but the statutes concerning LPs and LLLPs do not forbid such foreclosure, and Georgia courts have allowed foreclosure by a judgment creditor of a limited partnership interest. There are no restrictions on a judgment creditor who is seeking to satisfy his judgment against a shareholder's shares in a corporation.

SHOULD GEORGIA RESIDENTS FORM THEIR LLCS IN OTHER STATES?

It is no secret that many businesses headquartered in Georgia have used the corporate laws of other states for many, many years. For example, The Coca Cola Company is a Delaware corporation and so is Home Depot. Why? Delaware law gives management and officers certain rights and powers that these corporations find desirable, and such rights and powers for management and officers are not as favorable under Georgia law. Another reason that Delaware law is chosen is that Delaware is viewed as an innovator, and Delaware law is used by a large number of people, including attorneys, and they have become comfortable with it.

How significant is it that the laws of Tennessee, Delaware, Nevada, and certain other states provide that the exclusive remedy for a judgment creditor outside of bankruptcy is a charging order?

Remember that under Georgia law, a charging order is not the exclusive remedy for a judgment creditor. However, in a number of states, including Tennessee, Delaware, Nevada, and Arizona, the charging order is the exclusive remedy available to a judgment creditor. For example, if a member of a Tennessee LLC is at fault in a terrible car wreck and the injured party sues the member and gets a judgment that exceeds the member's automobile liability insurance coverage, the injured person—now the judgment creditor—can get a charging order. The judgment creditor takes the charging order to the LLC, and if the LLC intends to distribute any money to the debtor-member, it must instead pay that money to the judgment creditor until the judgment is paid in full. If the other members of the LLC are friendly with the member who got sued, they may delay distributions from the LLC to frustrate the judgment creditor, and the judgment creditor may agree to a greatly reduced lump-sum payment.

However, as explained above, once a member files for bankruptcy, state law and any provisions of an LLC's operating agreement that limit the rights of a creditor to a charging order or that require the consent of the other LLC's members to admit a bankruptcy trustee as member are not effective. Moreover, bankruptcy courts have held that under no circumstances can a bankruptcy trustee be prohibited from taking the interest of a member in an SMLLC. So states that limit a judgment creditor's remedy to a charging order are *primarily* only advantageous to a member who has not filed bankruptcy.

While it is true that Georgia's statute does give judgment creditors other remedies, including garnishment, the statute also prohibits the big remedies of foreclosure and sale of an LLC interest, interference in management, and dissolution of an LLC. Accordingly, whether you should form an LLC in Georgia or in a state where a charging order is the exclusive remedy for judgment creditors outside bankruptcy is a pretty close call. However, there are factors other than the "charging order as the exclusive remedy" that could make Georgia the preferred state.

Other issues besides charging orders to consider in deciding whether to form an LLC in a state other than Georgia.

An additional item to consider when deciding whether to form an LLC in Tennessee, Delaware, or Nevada, instead of Georgia, is the Full Faith and Credit Clause of the US Constitution. If a Georgia resident formed a Tennessee LLC, a Georgia creditor got a judgment against the Georgia resident, including a charging order and garnishment, it seems that the creditor should be able to take the Georgia judgment and charging order and garnishment to Tennessee and have the Tennessee courts apply the judgment, charging order, and garnishment to the Tennessee LLC. The result is that the Tennessee LLC does not help the Georgia resident. That is almost exactly what happened in the 2012 case of *In re Inman*, except the states involved were Florida and Colorado.

CASE STUDY: FULL FAITH AND CREDIT CLAUSE FOR LLCs

In Re Inman, 2012 WL 2390359

- Mr. and Mrs. Inman lived in Florida and got divorced in 2008. As part of the divorce decree, Inman agreed to pay his wife $1 million in alimony.

- The divorce settlement agreement provided that Mrs. Inman would secure a lien on her husband's ownership interest in two LLCs and an LLLP, all of which were formed under Colorado law: West Greenly Associates, LLC, Premise Real Estate, LLC, and Inman Family Enterprises, LLLP.

- When Inman stopped paying his wife's alimony, her attorney filed a petition with a Florida court, and the Florida judge issued a charging order that created a lien on Inman's Colorado LLCs and LLLP.

- Mrs. Inman filed the charging order in a Colorado district court and the Colorado court entered a charging order lien on Mr. Inman's interests in his LLC and LLP in favor of his ex-wife for $617,587.00.

- Before any money was paid to his wife, Inman filed for Chapter 11 bankruptcy relief.

- When Mrs. Inman was notified that her ex-husband had filed bankruptcy, she sent copies of the Florida judgment, the Colorado judgment ordering the charging order lien, and the divorce settlement agreement to the bankruptcy court.

- The bankruptcy court held that the Florida judgment was and remained a final judgment for the purposes of the Colorado proceedings, and further held that the charging liens entered by the Colorado court were, themselves, entitled to full faith and credit of the bankruptcy court.

- Therefore, Mrs. Inman was entitled, as a secured claim, to the interest of the value of the charging order lien issued by the Colorado court.

Another consideration when deciding whether to form an LLC in Tennessee, Delaware, or Nevada, instead of forming a Georgia LLC, is that the new out-of-state LLC will be subject to *all* the laws of the selected state. It is easy to form an LLC in states such as Tennessee, Nevada, or Delaware. There are many nonlawyer companies that advertise on the Internet and radio that will form an out-of-state LLC for $400 or less. In addition, the secretary of state offices in Nevada, Delaware, and other states have made their websites so user-friendly that anyone—with or without any special knowledge or legal training—can form an LLC in fifteen minutes or less. However, you will need to have an attorney in Nevada or Delaware to draft the operating agreement and keep you abreast of all the law changes in Nevada or Delaware year after year. Also, your out-of-state LLC will need to file income tax returns in the state of formation. Finally, if the out-of-state LLC owns property or conducts business in Georgia, the LLC will have to be registered and qualified to do business within the state of Georgia.

STRUCTURING FOR CHARGING ORDERS OUTSIDE OF BANKRUPTCY

In most cases, distributions of money from an LLC to the members are made pro rata among the members. So if the LLC makes a distribution of money to its members and one of the members has a judgment creditor with a charging order, the judgment creditor receives that member's distribution. A creditor with a changing order can sit and wait for distributions to be made from the LLC.

The other members, who do not have a charging order against them, may not want to wait for the creditor to go away or for the debtor-member to settle with the judgment creditor. The other members may want to take distributions now. Usually, creditors are patient and have the luxury of time. One solution to work around this issue is for each member to form a separate LLC to hold his or her membership interest so that the charging order would be against the LLC held by the individual debtor.

To illustrate, assume that John, Fred, and Sally are all doctors, that they are the three equal members of JFS Medical Practice, LLC, and that a creditor has won a judgment against John because of a bad real estate deal in which he was involved. The judgment creditor can get a charging order against John's interest in JFS Medical Practice, LLC, and then wait for distributions to be made from the LLC to its members. If Fred and Sally are friendly with John, they may decide to withhold distributions to put pressure on the creditor, and John may ask Fred and Sally not to make distributions. Fred and Sally may delay distributions for a while, but they may eventually need to make a distribution, thereby paying the judgment creditor John's one-third share of the distribution. However, if John, Fred, and Sally each have their own LLC, and those LLCs own the interests in JFS Medical Practice, LLC, then JFS Medical Practice, LLC can make distributions without the creditor getting John's one-third share, because that share will go to John's personal LLC. The judgment creditor will have to get a charging order against John's LLC, and then John and the judgment creditor can negotiate without involving Sally and Fred.

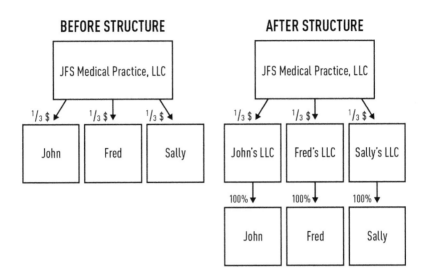

STRUCTURE TO ACHIEVE FRACTIONALIZATION

An important concept in asset-protection planning is called *fraction-alization*. This is the process of cutting something into pieces to make the pieces less valuable. Assume that someone, call him Bob, owns timberland worth $700,000 in Decatur County, Georgia (that is in southwest Georgia for everyone who lives in Atlanta). Assume Bob is in a bad auto accident, that the injured party wins a big judgment against Bob, and that the judgment amount still outstanding after Bob's auto insurance has run out is $600,000. The judgment creditor will be able to satisfy the judgment by selling Bob's timberland. But what would be the result if, two years before the accident, Bob had transferred the timberland to an LLC with the members being Bob (49 percent), his wife Hilda (49 percent), his son Frank (1 percent) and his daughter Susan (1 percent)? Assume that the LLC operating agreement requires 99 percent of the members to agree to admit a new partner, make distributions, sell timber, and sell the land.

Outside of bankruptcy, the judgment creditor only has the ability to collect money if and when money would otherwise have been paid to Bob. Not a good result for the judgment creditor, especially if the next harvest of timber is scheduled five years out. After a couple of years of getting nothing, the judgment creditor may be inclined to take a fraction (no pun intended) of the $600,000.

Inside bankruptcy, even if the bankruptcy trustee is able to convince the bankruptcy judge that the operating agreement is not an executory contract so that the trustee becomes a 49 percent member of the LLC, the trustee still cannot force a sale of the timber or the land or force a distribution of money, since a vote of 99 percent of the members is required.

INCORRECT CLAIM ON INTERNET: A JUDGMENT CREDITOR WHO HOLDS A CHARGING ORDER WILL HAVE TO PAY INCOME TAX ON A SHARE OF THE PROFITS OF THE LLC.

A charging order directs an LLC to pay a judgment creditor the money that otherwise would be due to the member who owes the creditor. Most LLCs are taxed like partnerships, with the result being that the LLC does not pay tax, and the members report their share of the LLC's income on their individual income tax returns (IRS Form 1040). Members of an LLC must pay income tax on their share of the LLC's income, even if the LLC does not make distributions to the members.

Some people claim that a creditor's ability to get money from the LLC via a charging order means that the creditor has, in effect, become a member and, consequently, must pay income tax on the debtor-member's share of the LLC's income. These people go on to claim that it is disadvantageous for a creditor to get a charging order because the creditor may have to pay income tax without getting any money. This is not correct. Only when a creditor becomes an assignee or member of the LLC will the creditor be subject to income tax. *See* Internal Revenue Service Revenue Ruling 77–137. A charging order is like a lien; it does not make the judgment creditor a member or even an assignee.

CHAPTER 7 RECAP:

- LLCs are the preferred business and investment entity in Georgia.

- A charging order is not the exclusive remedy of a judgment creditor in Georgia, but Georgia law does prohibit a judgment creditor from (a) interfering in the management of an LLC, (b) causing the dissolution of an LLC, and (c) foreclosing on a member's LLC interest. In this regard, Georgia law does not distinguish between SMLLCs and MMLLCs ... but, if possible, avoid SMLLCs.

- Once a member of an LLC files bankruptcy, the only way to keep the bankruptcy trustee from becoming a member of the LLC is to show that the LLC's operating agreement is an "executory contract," and that might be difficult. Thus, if possible, structure the LLC so that no member has 50 percent or more.

- All things considered, a Georgia MMLLC may be preferable to an out-of-state LLC. But a Georgia LLP may be an even better choice.

C H A P T E R   8

ASSETS THAT ARE EXEMPT FROM CREDITORS IN GEORGIA: A SHORT LIST

In Georgia, there are certain assets and income that the law declares to be exempt from creditors. In general, Georgia law exempts a certain amount or type of a person's assets and income from creditors to allow him or her to be able to support him- or herself and family members who are dependent on him or her. Also, the government encourages people to save for retirement, so there are laws that exempt certain retirement accounts from the reach of creditors.

The basic idea behind exempting certain assets and income is this: If a person's creditors are allowed to take all of his assets and income, the government's welfare programs will have to pay for the support of the debtor and family members who are dependent on him or her, typically a spouse and children under eighteen years of age. Implicit here is the notion that creditors should bear part of the blame or responsibility for *voluntarily* dealing with a person who is unable to pay his or her debts because the creditors should have done a better job investigating the debtor's ability to pay when the creditors *voluntarily* extended credit to the debtor. Think about credit-card companies, for example—they seem to do very little due diligence before issuing a credit card.

But what about someone who *involuntarily* deals with a debtor, like the friend of mine who was injured in a car wreck, and the driver at fault had no assets and no insurance? Even in that case, the law exempts the same amount of the negligent driver's income and assets to support himself and his family. Why? The law (a.k.a. our government and society) is telling us, even in this situation, that you must take care of yourself and you must protect your own assets. Prudent planning requires you to have insurance to protect against harm caused by a person with little or no assets or insurance.

There are two sets of rules concerning income and assets that are exempt from creditors: (1) the rules that apply to a person who has not filed bankruptcy (outside bankruptcy); and (2) the rules that apply to a person who has filed bankruptcy (inside bankruptcy). The fact that there are two sets of rules that apply to exempt assets should not be surprising. In chapter 5, we explained that the Georgia Uniform Fraudulent Transfer rules apply to a person outside of bankruptcy, but once that person files for bankruptcy, the bankruptcy code has its own special set of rules that deal with fraudulent transfers. In chapter 6, we explained that the bankruptcy code has a special rule that allows the bankruptcy trustee to challenge transfers made to self-settled trusts within the ten years leading up to the bankruptcy filing. Chapter 7 explains the different rules that apply to judgment creditors of an LLC member outside of bankruptcy and the rules that apply to an LLC member who is inside bankruptcy.

Federal bankruptcy law treats everyone the same, whether a person lives in Florida, Georgia, Tennessee, or wherever—with one important exception: The bankruptcy code sets forth a list of assets that are exempt for everyone, regardless of the state in which a person resides, *but* the bankruptcy code gives each state the option to "opt out" and, instead, require residents of a given state to accept that state's particular list of exempt assets and income. Most states, including Georgia, have "opted out" of the bankruptcy code's list of exempt assets and have come up with their own unique list. Some of the states that have "opted out" have generous lists of exempt assets, while other states exempt far fewer assets from the reach of creditors.

O. J. Simpson's move from California to Florida was reportedly motivated by Florida's generous exempt-asset list. Recall that Simpson was acquitted in the murder trial of Nicole Simpson and Ron Goldman—but lost the civil trial. The court awarded the Goldman family a $33.5 million judgment against Simpson in the civil trial. In Florida, a resident's home (called a "homestead" under the law)—regardless of value—is exempt from creditor process. Simpson reportedly bought a $500,000 home in Florida and was able to keep that $500,000 free from the judgment creditor! He also had a retirement account valued at $4 million, and the entire account was an exempt asset out of the reach of creditors.

Note: The bankruptcy code was changed in 2005, and one of the changes was intended to prevent people who have a judgment against them from moving to a debtor-friendly state like Florida, like O. J. Simpson did.

Georgia would not have been as generous to Mr. Simpson as Florida was. In Georgia, if a person has not filed bankruptcy, the following assets are exempt *to the extent specified below* from creditor process:

- **the beneficial interest of annuity contracts:** Pursuant to Georgia Code Section 33–28-7, the creditors of a Georgia resident who is a beneficiary of an annuity contract cannot reach the proceeds of the annuity *by attachment, garnishment, or legal process* unless the annuity was purchased, sold, or transferred with the intent to defraud creditors.

- **cash value of a life insurance policy:** Pursuant to Georgia Code Section 33–25–11(c), the creditors of a Georgia resident whose life is insured under a life insurance policy cannot reach the cash-surrender value *by attachment, garnishment, or legal process* unless the policy was purchased, sold, or transferred with the intent to defraud creditors.

- **individual retirement accounts (IRAs):** Pursuant to Georgia Code Section 18–4–22, the funds or benefits from an IRA shall be exempt from *garnishment* until paid or otherwise transferred to the beneficiary of the IRA, unless the garnishment is based upon a judgment for alimony or for child support.

- **401(k) and other interests in employer-sponsored qualified retirement plans:** Pursuant to Georgia Code Section 18-4-22, the funds or benefits from these retirement accounts shall be exempt from *garnishment* until paid or otherwise transferred to the beneficiary of the account, UNLESS the garnishment is based upon a judgment for alimony or for child support.

- However, under Georgia Code Section 53–12–80, if a spendthrift provision is included in a pension or retirement arrangement described in sections 401, 403, 404, 408, 408A, 409, 414, or 457 of the Internal Revenue Code of 1986, then the entire interest in the accounts can be protected from creditors, *except* where a claim is made pursuant to a qualified domestic-relations order by an ex-spouse in a divorce.

- **up to $21,500 of your primary residence, or $43,000 if the house is owned jointly with your spouse**

- **personal or real property in the amount of $5,000:** In addition to the $5,000, the debtor can also exempt up to $300 worth of kitchen and household furniture. § 44–13–41.

In Georgia, if a person files for bankruptcy relief, the following assets and income are exempt from creditors:

1. O.C.G.A. § 44-13-100(a)(8) permits the debtor to keep any unmatured life insurance contract, as long as it is not a credit life insurance policy. The Georgia code also permits the debtor to exempt up to $2,000 of the cash value of an unmatured life insurance policy.[6] Until recently, it appeared that O.C.G.A. § 33–25–11(c), a nonbankruptcy statute that prevents creditors from accessing any of the cash surrender value of a life insurance policy, might help debtors in Georgia to hold on to that cash value.[7] However, in a March 2012 decision, the Middle District of Georgia

6   O.C.G.A. § 44-13-100(a)(9).

7   Riser Adkisson, "Georgia Statutory Exemptions and Homestead," assetprotectionbook.com, Nov. 27, 2010, http://www.assetprotectionbook.com/forum/viewtopic.php?f=27&t=1196&sid=26e99df27c0ef759fa3eda07445a7b49.

Bankruptcy Court held that O.C.G.A. § 33–25–11(c) cannot be used to exempt property from the debtor's bankruptcy.[8]

2. Right to receive public benefits (e.g., Social Security, disability, Veteran's, unemployment).

3. Right to receive support maintenance (e.g., alimony, child support, payments under a pension or annuity, payments from an IRA) to the extent necessary for the support of you and your dependents.

4. Primary residence—current homestead exemption: $21,500; if debtor is married and the property is owned by only one spouse, the exemption may be increased to $43,000.

5. Motor vehicle (up to $5,000).

6. IRA (but not inherited IRAs) and qualified retirement plans.

Georgia's history is that of a pro-creditor state, so it is not surprising that Georgia law exempts few assets from creditor process. There are some states, like our neighbor Florida, that exempt many more assets than Georgia does, but you have to be a resident of Florida to avail yourself of Florida's exemptions.

CHAPTER 8 RECAP:

- The laws applicable to Georgia residents are very different from the laws of our neighboring states, so Georgia residents who engage in asset-

---

8   *In re Dean*, 470 B.R. 643, 648, (Bankr. M.D. Ga. 2012).

protection planning should not be looking to Nevada, Delaware, or even Florida or Tennessee.

- Certain assets that are exempt from creditors lose the exempt status once you file bankruptcy.

- Georgia is a "pro-creditor" state, so there are not many assets that are exempt from creditors.

CONTRACT CLAUSES THAT KEEP YOU OUT OF THE COURT SYSTEM AND MINIMIZE LIABILITY

A contract is a written agreement between two parties that explains the terms of the relationship between them. Important terms include: (a) the description of the services or goods to be provided; (b) when payment will be made for the goods or services; (c) how long the relationship will last; and (d) what happens in the event of a dispute between the parties. However, not all contracts are equal; some are good, some are bad, some are obtained from the Internet, and some are copied from other people.

This chapter examines how certain contract provisions can keep Georgia residents out of court and minimize your liability to others.

Most of my clients are people who are on the paying end of contracts. That is, they have the money and they pay other people to do something, like perform a service, construct a building, repair something, or produce a product. The party who is paying for the goods and services only has to pay money to complete their job of the contract—a pretty simple job assuming they have the money. The other party on a contract has the big responsibility: Do the task or produce the product. The party who is paying money will likely not default. The other party is most likely to default by failing to deliver part or all of the product or service. Since the other party may default—and then complain for not getting paid (that is, file a lawsuit), we include contract provisions for our clients to try to avoid court and minimize liability and damages.

HERE ARE EXAMPLES OF CONTRACT PROVISIONS TO AVOID COURT AND MINIMIZE LIABILITY AND DAMAGES:

1. Arbitration provisions. These provisions require (a) a dispute between the parties to be settled in a private setting (not a court of law) by a person who has expertise in the matter being disputed (known as the "arbitrator") and (b) the loser to pay the winner's attorney fees. Businesses and people who have a lot to lose prefer that claims against them be settled by arbitration, as opposed to being decided by a judge and jury at the courthouse. There are many companies that provide arbirtators and facilities to people who wish to settle their disputes in a private setting and not at the courthouse. Many of these companies hire experienced attorneys who are actively practicing law and attorneys who are retired.

WHY CHOOSE ARBITRATION?

- A lawsuit can take years to reach a resolution, but arbitration can be finished in several months.
- Attorney fees are minimized.

- The loser in a lawsuit almost never has to pay the attorney fees of the winner, so many people and their attorneys have no real risk or downside to filing a lawsuit. However, an arbitration contract can require the loser to pay the winner's attorney fees, thereby creating a disincentive to making a claim with little or no merit.

- A lawsuit is open to anyone who wants to examine the court records and attend the trial and hearings, so even false allegations about you can be spread through gossip, the Internet, TV, Twitter, radio, newspapers, Facebook, LinkedIn, etc. No doubt, many people file lawsuits just to embarrass or harass the other party into a settlement. However, the arbitration process is private and there are no filings at the courthouse.

- There is a notion that juries and some judges create their own "justice" in favor of the "little guy" against businesses, insurance companies, and people with financial resources and assets.

- The arbitrator is not required to follow the rationale of prior court cases (known as "legal precedent") decided by judges and jury.

Employers often have arbitration clauses in employment contracts with employees, and most construction contracts have arbitration clauses. However, arbitration clauses are not permitted as a way to settle all issues in Georgia, so in certain situations the law requires that certain contractual disputes be handled in the court system. For example, landlords who want to dispossess a tenant must file a court action to get the tenant removed. Also, remember that arbitration contracts are written agreements between people who are in a business relationship, so you cannot force a person who has a claim against you outside of a business relationship into arbitration. For example, if you injure someone in an automobile accident, you cannot require the injured party to arbitrate the claim; the injured party is permitted to use the court system and file a lawsuit against you.

2. Employment contracts. An employment contract between an employee and the company he or she works for should (a) describe and list the duties of the employee; (b) describe the employee's compensation and benefits, if any; (c) prohibit the employee from soliciting the company's customers when the employee leaves and goes to work for a competitor; (d) authorize the employer to perform credit and criminal background checks on the employee, (e) explain vacation and sick leave; and (f) require that claims by the employee against the company be settled in arbitration.

Most companies do not have employment contracts with their employees because companies think that an employment agreement is expensive and not necessary. Neither is true. A "template" or form agreement where you fill in each employee's name, salary, and duties can be used, so that you are not required to pay your attorney to draft a new agreement for each employee.

The best thing about employment agreements is that they establish, in writing, the relationship between the company and employee. This is called "setting expectations," and in big companies the human resources department sets the expectations with employees by going over their employment contracts with them. Perhaps the best way to avoid a dispute is to make sure both parties understand what is expected of them and what they will get out of the relationship. If you can avoid a dispute, you avoid a claim against your assets and income. While setting expectations is important between employees and companies, setting expectations as a way to avoid disputes is important in every relationship: student and teacher; husband and wife; business partners; clients and businesses, etc.

3. Contract that eliminates your liability for negligence. Generally, if you are negligent in performing your duties to another person or company, you can be sued—or if you have an arbitration provision in the contract, a claim will be filed with the arbitrator. However, you could use a contract that provides that you can be liable for damages *only if* you are "grossly negligent or totally careless" or *only if* you intentionally try to damage the other party. Professional investment managers often have contracts that provide that the manager is only liable for "gross negligence or wanton and careless behavior."

Under Georgia law, professionals such as lawyers and doctors cannot have contracts that eliminate their liability for negligence, so professionals have to use other strategies to protect their assets. A lawyer shall not attempt to exonerate himself from or limit his liability to his client for his personal malpractice.[9]

In Georgia, professionals may not contractually limit the duty to use the reasonable degree of care and skill required in the practice of the profession.[10] The court holds that the waiver is against public policy because the general assembly places a minimum standard on the medical profession to which they cannot fall below. According to the statute governing medical professionals in Georgia, a medical professional must bring a reasonable degree of care and skill and any injury resulting from a want of such care and skill shall be a tort for which recovery may be had. This is one reason that professionals typically have substantial liability (malpractice) insurance.

4. Contract that limits the dollar amount of damages. There are contracts that specify that an injured party can only recover a certain amount of damages. These contracts try to cap damages. These

---

9   Georgia Rules of Professional Conduct, Rule 1.8(h).

10   Emory University v. Porubainsky, 248 Ga. 391 (1981).

contract provisions are found most often in commercial real estate leases where a business is leasing space in a building. A common provision limits liability of the landlord only to the extent of the landlord's equity in the building, with "equity" being defined as the value of the building minus the debt on the building. Since most commercial-building owners keep high amounts of debt on their buildings, most of the time there is little "equity" in a building. Thus, the landlord's liability exposure is small according to the contract. It is not clear if these clauses are valid, but they exist in many commercial real estate leases and at a minimum are a hurdle that the tenant must overcome.

5. Contract that requires the loser to pay the winning party's legal fees. Some people file lawsuits and claims in arbitration that have little or no merit, because the person making the claim has little to lose. You have seen the attorney advertisements on TV or on billboards where the attorney says that the client owes them nothing if they don't recover money for their client. Under Georgia law, it is very difficult to get a judge to order that the losing party pay the attorney fees of the winning party. However, if you are in a business relationship with another party, such as an employee, you can use a contract that requires the loser to pay the winner's attorney fees. This will normally make people think twice about filing a lawsuit, because the attorney fees could be substantial.

What the heck, if they don't have to pay the attorney unless their is a recovery, why not file the lawsuit. Under Georgia law, there are limits on the amount of attorney fees that a loser can be forced to pay. For example, if a bank or other lender sues to collect money due under a promissory note, attorney fees that can be recouped by the bank are limited to generally 15 percent of the amount of the loan.

Georgia courts have extended the 15 percent cap on attorney fees to amounts due under real estate leases. Many people think that it is unfair that a landlord can only collect 15 percent of the rent due as attorney fees, since it may take a lot of money in attorney fees to deal with a deadbeat or uncooperative client, or to dispossess a tenant.

> *Hudson's Tip:* Landlords should get at least a couple months' rent for the security deposit and they should make the tenant pay for part or all of the insurance on the house/space. Also, do a background check on the tenant and verify employment and salary.

6. Privacy and Nondisclosure Contracts. A privacy and nondisclosure contract provides that the parties cannot make disparaging statements about the business relationship to other people. So, even if a person you do business with gets mad at you and does not file a lawsuit, he or she may want to "get even" with you by posting disparaging and perhaps untrue things about your business or you on the Internet. In such instances, these contracts can help protect your business and, therefore, your assets.

CERTAIN CONTRACT PROVISIONS ARE NOT PERMITTED IN GEORGIA.

As mentioned, there are certain situations where Georgia law does not allow parties to use contracts to require arbitration, limit damages, limit attorney fees, etc. in setting the terms of their business relationship. In those situations, the public policy of Georgia is that one party needs extra protection as in the case of residential tenants. The feeling is that people who rent a house or an apartment have little or no bargaining position with landlords, so Georgia law steps in to make sure the tenants are protected. The following is a list of contract provisions that either are not permitted in residential lease contracts or must be modified:

- The lease contract cannot contain an arbitration clause requiring arbitration for personal injury or wrongful death that may occur on the property.

- The lease contract cannot waive the landlord's duty to repair.

- The lease contract cannot waive the landlord's liability for the duty to repair or defective construction.

- It cannot waive housing-code ordinances.

- It cannot waive compliance with dispossessory or distress procedures permitted or provisions governing security deposits.

- It cannot delegate duty to repair on an independent contractor.

- It can require a tenant to pay the landlord's attorney fees if a landlord hires an attorney to enforce the lease, *but* the lease must also provide a provision that makes the landlord responsible for the tenant's attorney fees if the landlord breaches the lease. (Reciprocal.)

- Attorney fees for unpaid rent are subject to O.C.G.A. § 13-1-11, which provides a statutory cap of 15 percent.

- Attorney fees for other claims not dealing with the "indebtedness" of a tenant are not required to fall under the 15 percent statutory cap.

- The landlord is not prohibited from requiring tenants to purchase renter's insurance to cover tenant's personal property.

- An exculpatory or indemnity clause attempting to void the landlord's liability for negligence, especially the liability for defects in construction, is void, as it is against public policy in both commercial and residential leases.

The following is a list of contract provisions that either are not permitted in commercial lease contracts or must be modified:

- Attorney fees for unpaid rent are subject to O.C.G.A. § 13–1–11, which provides a statutory cap of 15 percent.

- Attorney fees for other claims not dealing with the "indebtedness" of a tenant are not required to fall under the 15 percent statutory cap.

- The lease cannot contain an exculpatory or indemnity clause attempting to avoid the landlord's liability for negligence.

- The lease may contain a provision having the landlord purchase insurance and having the tenant pay for the insurance premiums.

  - The court holds that "it has been recognized by numerous authorities that *where parties to a business transaction mutually agree that insurance will be provided as a part of the bargain, such agreement must be construed as providing mutual exculpation to the bargaining parties who must be deemed to have agreed to look solely to the insurance in the event of loss* and not to liability on the part of the opposing party."[11]

CHAPTER 9 RECAP:

1. Documenting your business agreement with another person in a written contract is the best way to avoid misunderstandings that can lead to disputes—that can lead to lawsuits. Lawsuits are good for lawyers but are terrible for a person who has money and assets and a lot to lose. A lawsuit is not really a bad thing for someone who had no assets and nothing to lose. In fact, a lot of people with nothing to lose join up with lawyers and file lawsuits as a way to make money. Look at all the advertisements.

2. There are simple contract provisions that in most instances can keep you out of the court system and can reduce or eliminate your liability exposure.

---

11   Pettus v. APC Inc., 162 Ga. App 804 (1982).

C H A P T E R   1 0

SPECIFIC SUGGESTIONS AND TECHNIQUES FOR GEORGIANS

This chapter offers some specific suggestions and techniques for Georgia residents to protect their assets.

1. NEVER DO BUSINESS IN YOUR PERSONAL NAME. ALWAYS CONDUCT YOUR BUSINESS ACTIVITIES THROUGH A SEPARATE LEGAL ENTITY SUCH AS AN LLC OR A CORPORATION.

The reason is that if there is a dispute with a customer or tenant or the like, you want the dispute to be between the other party and your business entity (not *you*). For example, assume you own a rental house, the deed is in your name, and you rent the house to tenants. You should form an LLC, the deed for the house should be in the name of the LLC, and the lease agreement with the tenant should be between the LLC and the tenant. This way, if the tenant or a guest of the tenant is injured at the property, the dispute (most likely a lawsuit) will be between the tenant and your LLC—not the tenant and you.

> **Hudson's Tip:** It is always best to form the LLC or corporation when the rental house is acquired, so that your LLC or corporation is on the deed from the start, instead of you having the deed in your name and then you deed the property to the LLC or corporation. The reasons are that when you deed a rental house to an LLC or corporation, you might negate the title insurance that you have on the property, there might be income tax consequences associated with the transfer, and your security deed with the bank that loaned you money to buy the house may have a "due-on-sale" clause that allows the bank to call the loan immediately. Also make sure the homeowners-insurance policy lists the LLC as the "insured" and "owner," not you.

If the tenant wins the lawsuit with your LLC and gets a court judgment against your LLC, only the asset(s) of the LLC can be used to satisfy the judgment. If the LLC only owns one house and there is only $10,000 of equity in the house, that is all the tenant will get. Your personal assets and other income cannot be reached by the tenant.

2. ACQUIRE A PERSONAL "UMBRELLA" LIABILITY INSURANCE POLICY.

A personal "umbrella" liability policy kicks in only if your auto insurance or your homeowners insurance is not adequate to cover the damages. Assume (a) you are in an automobile accident that is your fault because you were texting, e-mailing, or talking on the phone and were distracted, (b) the person you injured has a permanent disability, and you are liable for a loss that is $600,000 greater than your auto insurance coverage. Even though you might not have $600,000 in the bank to pay the judgment, the person you injured can take money from your future earnings and wages. A personal "umbrella" policy will kick in when the limits of your automobile policy have been exceeded. So if you had a $1,000,000 umbrella policy, the policy would pay the $600,000 loss.

Umbrella policies are inexpensive, usually around a couple hundred dollars for $1,000,000 of coverage. Personal umbrella policies usually do not cover liability for business or commercial losses. For example, a personal umbrella policy probably will not cover injury to a tenant in a rental house because the rental activity is a business activity, not a personal activity. Check with your insurance agent.

3. COMMERCIAL/BUSINESS LIABILITY INSURANCE.

Be sure that you have commercial (business) insurance that covers the activities that could cause the most damage to another person. Go over the particulars of the policy with your agent to make sure what activities are covered and which activities are excluded. You can get an umbrella policy for your commercial and business liabilities policies.

Aside from protecting valuable assets and future income, having adequate liability insurance can be a selling point to the people with whom you do business. Having adequate liability insurance lets your customer know that you are a serious businessperson and that you care about them.

> **Hudson's Tip:** It may sound like it, but I am not a liability insurance agent and I have no interest in having you purchase insurance that you do not need. For example, I personally select high deductible limits on my business, health, auto and homeowners insurance because (a) doing so lowers my premiums and (b) I primarily purchase insurance to cover big losses that would substantially set me back or wipe out my assets. The "deductible" is the dollar amount of a loss that you have to pay out of your pocket before the insurance starts to pay. When you shop for liability coverage, check out the price discounts from increasing your deductible.

4. GET ASSETS OUT OF YOUR NAME.

Consider transferring assets to trusts for the benefit of your spouse and children. The trust should include a provision that if you and your spouse are no longer married or living together, then your spouse will cease to be a beneficiary and trustee of the trust. The trust can be an investor and/or partner in business ventures with you, or the trust can loan you or your businesses money. To illustrate, assume you invest in real estate. You have $150,000 in an account at Merrill Lynch, you are married, you have a son who is twelve, and a daughter who is nine. The money in the Merrill Lynch account is money that you have saved, you only intend to use it for investments, and you plan on adding to the account over the years. If you were to be sued, the money in the Merrill Lynch account would be something that would be very attractive; we call this "low-hanging fruit." You could establish a trust for your spouse and your children, and your spouse could be the trustee of the trust, however, it might be better for someone like your brother, sister, or parent to be the trustee. The trust could continue to have an account at Merrill Lynch and make investments in stocks and bonds. The trust could also invest as a partner in your business ventures or it could make loans to your businesses. The result is that you have removed assets from your name, yet kept them available to your family.

5. HOLD INVESTMENT ASSETS SUCH AS TAXABLE STOCK ACCOUNTS IN LLCs, WITH ONE OR MORE PERSONS SUCH AS YOUR SPOUSE AND CHILDREN— OR IN TRUST FOR THE BENEFIT OF CHILDREN.

Some people may not feel comfortable putting most of their assets in trust for the benefit of their spouse and children. An alternative is to put a smaller number of assets into the trusts and to put substantial investment assets into an LLC or limited partnership. The LLC would be structured so that you and a family member, other than your spouse, must agree on decisions affecting the LLC, particularly the decision to take assets out of the LLC. The reason that the LLC is structured so that you must have the consent of someone else is so that if you are the loser in a lawsuit, you do not have the ability to take valuable investment assets out of the LLC to give to the judgment creditor. Care must be taken in funding these entities or else disastrous income tax results can occur.

Again, you must make "low-hanging fruit" difficult for judgment creditors to reach. One of the best ways to do this is to take an asset that you own, break it up into separate pieces, keep one piece yourself, and give the other pieces to people who you trust and wish to benefit. When you create an LLC, put valuable assets into it, and then give parts of the LLC to family members, you make the part of the LLC that you keep virtually worthless to a future judgment creditor. Think about it: What good is an interest in an LLC to a judgment creditor if the creditor has to get the consent of your family members to take money out of the LLC?

6. INCLUDE ARBITRATION PROVISIONS IN ALL CONTRACTS.

Insist on contracts that (a) require that disputes be settled by binding arbitration, (b) require that the arbitrator be someone who has substantial knowledge and experience in your business, (c) do not allow the dispute to get into the court/lawsuit system, (d) require the losing party in the dispute to pay all attorney fees and costs, and (e) require that the arbitration be handled where you reside.

Most often, I represent people who put money into a business, and their business partner puts in little or no money, but instead operates the business or is otherwise required to perform and deliver a service or product. Put another way, my client's job is to put the money in the deal (so my client does not have much to do to uphold his or her end of the bargain) and the other party is supposed to do something, such as operate the business (so the partner has a lot to do/perform). The party who will likely breach the agreement or fail to perform is not going to be my client. When the other party breaches, we do not want to enter the court system (which seems set up for bad actors and is slow and unpredictable), and we want our legal fees to be paid by the person who makes the bogus claim.

7. NEVER HAVE EMPLOYEES PERFORM TASKS THAT CAN BE PERFORMED BY COURIERS OR DELIVERY SERVICES.

You can be held liable for accidents caused by your employees. You should not be liable for accidents by employees of the courier or delivery service.

8. PREPARE SIMPLE EMPLOYMENT CONTRACTS THAT REQUIRE ARBITRATION AND SET EXPECTATIONS REGARDING TIME OFF AND OVERTIME.

I have been in many meetings where important matters were discussed and people shook hands at the end of the meeting and were seemingly in agreement—yet after the meeting, the attendees had different understandings or interpretations about some of the key details that were "agreed to." I have seen this happen with smart, reasonable, and honest people. The best way to make sure that people truly understand and agree is to put the terms of the agreement in writing. This especially applies to employees. You should have an employment contract that details compensations, benefits, sick leave, and vacation and stipulates that any disputes will be settled by arbitration (not a court of law). Attached as Appendix D is a sample employment agreement.

9. KNOW WHO YOU ARE DOING BUSINESS WITH; KNOWLEDGE IS POWER.

Perhaps the best way to avoid a lawsuit with a business partner or associate is to know as much as possible about the person with whom you are considering doing business. Do a thorough investigation and background check of the proposed business associate/partner. Get the permission of the person to do a credit and criminal check on him or her. Find out the number of lawsuits the person has been involved in, either as a plaintiff or defendant. Many county and state governments have websites that allow you to search by name the lawsuits in which a person has been involved, the liens that have been filed by or against a person or entity, the real estate owned by the party, and mortgages owed by the party. Also, you should Google the person's name on Internet searches for additional information. Finally, there are services like LexisNexis Accurint® that offer a menu of searches for fairly nominal fees.

I cannot tell you the number of people that I know who have been totally duped in a business deal because their business partner misrepresented who he or she was. Many times, the business partner does not perform adequately and/or takes money that was supposed to be used in the business enterprise. Are you going to sue the party? Lawsuits require significant sums for legal fees; the fraudster may file a bogus counterclaim that you have to defend against (causing you to spend more money in legal fees)—and lawsuits easily take one or more years to be concluded. Plus, assuming you get a judgment, collecting money from the fraudster is often like trying to collect money from a ghost. These people love lawsuits because they can hire a lawyer who can cause delay and frustrate you. These people have nothing to lose, you have everything to lose. The court system is a game with rules stacked against people with money and assets, however, if you prepare, you can refuse to pay the court system game.

Do business with people who check out, have substantial assets, and have been established for years. My experience is that people who have nothing or little to lose are more likely to do a poor job or to file a lawsuit against you. These types of people do not make good defendants in a lawsuit, because if you get a judgment against them, they have no assets—so you will collect little to nothing or they will file bankruptcy.

10. HAVE LEASE AGREEMENTS THAT ARE FAVORABLE TO YOU.

If you own a house or building and lease the property to tenants, you need a lease that is "pro-landlord"—that is, a lease that contains provisions that are most favorable to the landlord. Remember, Georgia law seeks to protect tenants, especially residential tenants, so the lease cannot be 100 percent in the landlord's favor. For example, to get rid of a tenant who does not pay and will not move out, Georgia law requires the landlord to file a lawsuit and get the sheriff to move the tenant's belongings out of the property. Attached as Appendix E is a sample pro-landlord residential real estate lease.

11. IF YOU OWN THE BUILDING AND LAND WHERE YOUR BUSINESS IS LOCATED, HAVE SEPARATE ENTITIES.

Create an LLC and transfer the real estate to it; we call it the "Land-Holding LLC." Then, create a separate LLC or S corporation that will own and operate the business; we call this the "Business LLC." An automobile dealership is a good example. There are many customers who visit the dealership every day, some are looking to buy cars, and some are coming to get their car serviced. In addition, the dealership has a lot of employees who come to the dealership daily, and other companies have employees that deliver products like auto parts to the dealership. If a customer, employee, or vendor is injured at the dealership, it would be best if the land and the building were owned by the land-holding LLC and the business were owned by the business LLC. If the business and the land were owned together, the injured party could use the business *and* the land to satisfy the injured party's damages. By separating the property and the business into separate LLCs, the property should be safe from the injured party (and his attorney). The land-holding LLC should enter into a lease with the business LLC. The lease should require the business LLC to pay a fair-market rent to the land-holding LLC—and the business LLC should also be required to have insurance and be responsible for any injuries to persons who visit the dealership. There may also be some income tax advantages to the payment of rent by the business LLC to the land-holding LLC.

12. ENTER INTO PRENUPTIAL AGREEMENTS.

Most prenuptial agreements are entered into between people who have been married before and do not want to go through the gut-wrenching, unpredictable experience of a divorce. Plus they want to avoid the high attorney fees—another dreadful byproduct of a divorce. Prenuptial agreements allow the parties to divorce with agreed-upon results and few or no attorney fees.

13. CREATE TRUSTS UNDER YOUR LAST WILL & TESTAMENT TO PROTECT YOUR CHILDREN'S INHERITANCE.

The inheritance that you leave to your children should be held in trusts that are crafted to give your children access and use of the inheritance, and at the same time keep the inheritance protected from their creditors, including an ex-son-in-law or an ex-daughter-in-law. These trusts can be structured to stay in place for the entire life of your children and pass at a child's death to your grandchildren. To illustrate how the trusts would work, assume you have two children, a son, Bill Jr., and a daughter, Sallie. After you are deceased, Bill Jr. and Sallie are the trustees of Bill Jr.'s trust and they are also the trustees of Sallie's trust. Bill Jr. has the sole authority to make investment decisions of his trust, and Sallie has the same authority for her trust. However, only Sallie has the power to authorize distributions from Bill Jr.'s trust to Bill Jr., and Bill Jr. alone has the power to authorize distributions to Sallie from her trust. When Sallie dies, her trust passes to her children, and when Bill Jr. dies, his trust passes to his children.

The assets in Bill Jr.'s trust and Sallie's trust should be protected from their respective creditors, yet Bill Jr. and Sallie are involved in the management of the trusts and have access to use of the money.

CHAPTER 10 RECAP:

1. There are many techniques you can use to protect your assets.

2. However, you must take action after finishing this book and actually implement the techniques that are appropriate for your situation.

CHAPTER 11

DECIDING TO REDUCE OR ELIMINATE LIABILITY AND/OR MALPRACTICE INSURANCE

Below is a recap of the money I spend every year on insurance:

a)	medical	$20,000 (for a family of five)
b)	auto	$1,800 (for two cars)
c)	homeowners	$5,000
d)	umbrella	$600 ($2,000,000 coverage)
e)	office property and casualty	$5,000
f)	malpractice	$14,500 ($2,000,000 coverage)
g)	term life insurance	$9,120 ($4,000,000 coverage)
h)	cyber crime and employee theft	$3,200
		$59,220

Take a moment to itemize and tally the money *you* spend annually on insurance. For everyone except doctors, who have very expensive malpractice insurance, the most expensive insurance coverages are medical insurance, homeowners insurance, and life insurance. Auto, umbrella, malpractice, and property and casualty insurance are the least expensive items. This is because the "typical" businessperson is less likely to file a claim (or at most a relatively small claim) for causing injury to another person or that person's property. Also, "umbrella" insurance only applies when your primary liability insurance coverage is not adequate to cover the claim against you. Since the typical business person rarely has a claim that exceeds his primary liability insurance, umbrella insurance is very inexpensive.

I have heard some practitioners in the asset-protection "business" tell people that if you pay them a lot of money for their "asset protection package," you will be able to quit paying malpractice and liability insurance. In my opinion, that is terrible advice and is merely the way these type of "planners" justify the outrageous fees for their "asset protection package." I have insurance for malpractice and liability for three reasons: (1) to protect my assets and income, (2) I feel that I have an obligation to protect my clients and people I may injure if I make a big mistake or cause an accident, and (3) people and businesses will not want to do business with me if I do not have adequate insurance. In fact, some people require that you have a certain amount and type of insurance as a condition of doing business with them. Again, instead of eliminating coverage, you should be able to reduce the cost of your insurance by using high deductibles—and you might be able to reduce the amount of coverage by implementing some of the steps outlined in this book.

CHAPTER 11 RECAP:

1. Doing away with your liability insurance is not a realistic goal for undertaking asset-protection planning.

2. However, asset-protection planning combined with liability insurance will increase the likelihood that you will keep your assets, especially if the claim against you is not covered by your insurance or you do not have insurance for the claim.

WHAT DO YOU DO IF YOU HAVE ALREADY BEEN SUED OR YOUR LIABILITIES EXCEED YOUR ASSETS?

1. Talk to an experienced attorney who has dealt with creditors and who knows what the creditor can do "outside of bankruptcy" and "inside of bankruptcy."

2. Do not send e-mails or letters or talk to nonlawyers about your situation because only conversations with your attorney are privileged and confidential. Communications with nonlawyers can be discovered by the creditor's attorney.

3. Don't assume the worst will happen. Creditors will often settle for a fraction (could be 20 percent, could be 70 percent) of the amount owed to them, especially if your attorney can present defenses to the claim.

MYTHS AND BOGUS CLAIMS ABOUT ASSET PROTECTION

Myth #1: Asset protection is transferring assets to offshore bank accounts. FALSE.

- Offshore bank accounts must be disclosed on your federal income tax return, and a judge can make you turn over the bank account to creditors.

Myth #2: You should start planning to protect your assets once someone has a claim against you. For example, you rear-end someone while driving and the accident is clearly your fault, the other driver is seriously injured, and then you transfer all your assets to your spouse. FALSE.

- As discussed in chapter 5, most transfers can be undone by someone who has a claim against you when you do not leave enough assets in your name to cover the claim or do not have enough insurance to cover the claim. Asset protection must be done *before* you have claims.

Myth #3: Asset-protection planning started about twenty years ago when small island countries, like the Cook Islands, passed favorable asset-protection laws. FALSE.

- Asset-protection planning has been around for centuries and has been practiced by sophisticated attorneys, accountants, and their clients long before the Cook Islands became a country.

Myth #4: Georgia residents need to form LLCs, corporations, and trusts in foreign countries or in states like Delaware, Nevada, and Florida to have effective asset-protection planning. FALSE.

- Moreover, some of the promoters who recommend that you use the foreign entities are not attorneys, and they do not have malpractice insurance if they give you bad advice. Many attorneys who would recommend foreign entities are not licensed to practice law in these other states or countries—so how do they know the law? The short answer is that *they don't*.

Myth #5: You can hide assets. FALSE.

- Everyone has a financial history, and you cannot make that history disappear. The Internet has made it is easier than ever to locate a person's assets. For example, just about all states have their real estate deed and tax records online and also have online records for LLCs, partnerships, and corporations. Credit-reporting agencies and private investigators also have access to a wealth of information on you. In addition, there are illegitimate ways for people to get information on you, such as hacking your computer.

Myth #6: You must transfer all of the assets out of your name to do effective asset-protection planning. FALSE.

GEORGIA UNIFORM FRAUDULENT TRANSFERS ACT

§ 18–2–70: *Short Title*

This article shall be known and may be cited as the "Uniform Fraudulent Transfers Act."

§ 18–2–71: *Definitions*

As used in this article, the term:

(1) "Affiliate" means:

> *(A) A person who directly or indirectly owns, controls, or holds with power to vote, 20 percent or more of the outstanding voting securities of the debtor, other than a person who holds the securities:*

> > *(i) As a fiduciary or agent without sole discretionary power to vote the securities; or*

(ii) Solely to secure a debt, if the person has not exercised the power to vote;

(B) A corporation 20 percent or more of whose outstanding voting securities are directly or indirectly owned, controlled, or held with power to vote by the debtor or a person who directly or indirectly owns, controls, or holds with power to vote 20 percent or more of the outstanding voting securities of the debtor, other than a person who holds the securities:

(i) As a fiduciary or agent without sole power to vote the securities; or

(ii) Solely to secure a debt, if the person has not in fact exercised the power to vote;

(C) A person whose business is operated by the debtor under a lease or other agreement, or a person substantially all of whose assets are controlled by the debtor; or

(D) A person who operates the debtor's business under a lease or other agreement or controls substantially all of the debtor's assets.

(2) "Asset" means property of a debtor, but the term does not include:

(A) Property to the extent it is encumbered by a valid lien;

(B) Property to the extent it is generally exempt under non-bankruptcy law; or

(C) An interest in property held in tenancy by the entireties to the extent it is not subject to process by a creditor holding a claim against only one tenant.

(3) "Claim" means a right to payment, whether or not the right is reduced to judgment, liquidated, unliquidated, fixed, contingent, matured, unmatured, disputed, undisputed, legal, equitable, secured, or unsecured.

(4) "Creditor" means a person who has a claim.

(5) "Debt" means liability on a claim.

(6) "Debtor" means a person who is liable on a claim.

(7) "Insider" includes:

    (A) If the debtor is an individual:

        (i) A relative of the debtor or of a general partner of the debtor;

        (ii) A partnership in which the debtor is a general partner;

        (iii) A general partner in a partnership described in division (ii) of this subparagraph; or

        (iv) A corporation of which the debtor is a director, officer, or person in control;

    (B) If the debtor is a corporation:

    (i) A director of the debtor;

    (ii) An officer of the debtor;

    (iii) A person in control of the debtor;

    (iv) A partnership in which the debtor is a general partner;

(v) A general partner in a partnership described in division (iv) of this subparagraph; or

(vi) A relative of a general partner, director, officer, or person in control of the debtor;

(C) If the debtor is a partnership:

(i) A general partner in the debtor;

(ii) A relative of a general partner in, or a general partner of, or a person in control of the debtor;

(iii) Another partnership in which the debtor is a general partner;

(iv) A general partner in a partnership described in division (iii) of this subparagraph; or

(v) A person in control of the debtor;

(D) An affiliate, or an insider of an affiliate as if the affiliate were the debtor; and

(E) A managing agent of the debtor.

(8) "Lien" means a charge against or an interest in property to secure payment of a debt or performance of an obligation and includes a security interest created by agreement, a judicial lien obtained by legal or equitable process or proceedings, a common-law lien, or a statutory lien.

(9) "Person" means an individual, partnership, corporation, association, organization, government or governmental subdivision or agency, business trust, estate, trust, or any other legal or commercial entity.

(10) "Property" means anything that may be the subject of ownership.

(11) *"Relative" means an individual related by consanguinity within the third degree as determined by the common law, a spouse, or an individual related to a spouse within the third degree as so determined and includes an individual in an adoptive relationship within the third degree.*

(12) *"Transfer" means every mode, direct or indirect, absolute or conditional, voluntary or involuntary, of disposing of or parting with an asset or an interest in an asset and includes payment of money, release, lease, and creation of a lien or other encumbrance.*

(13) *"Valid lien" means a lien that is effective against the holder of a judicial lien subsequently obtained by legal or equitable process or proceedings.*

§ 18–2–72: When Debtor or Debtor Partnership is Insolvent

(a) A debtor is insolvent if the sum of the debtor's debts is greater than all of the debtor's assets, at a fair valuation.

(b) A debtor who is generally not paying his or her debts as they become due is presumed to be insolvent.

(c) A partnership is insolvent under subsection (a) of this Code section if the sum of the partnership's debts is greater than the aggregate of all of the partnership's assets, at a fair valuation, and the sum of the excess of the value of each general partner's nonpartnership assets over the partner's nonpartnership debts.

(d) Assets under this Code section do not include property that has been transferred, concealed, or removed with intent to hinder, delay, or defraud creditors or that has been transferred in a manner making the transfer voidable under this article.

(e) Debts under this Code section do not include an obligation to the extent it is secured by a valid lien on property of the debtor not included as an asset.

§ 18–2–73: When Value is Given for Transfer or Obligation

(a) Value is given for a transfer or an obligation if, in exchange for the transfer or obligation, property is transferred or an antecedent debt is secured or satisfied, but value does not include an unperformed promise made otherwise than in the ordinary course of the promisor's business to furnish support to the debtor or another person.

(b) For the purposes of paragraph (2) of subsection (a) of Code Section 18–2–74 and Code Section 18–2–75, a person gives a reasonably equivalent value if the person acquires an interest of the debtor in an asset pursuant to a regularly conducted, noncollusive foreclosure sale or execution of a power of sale for the acquisition or disposition of the interest of the debtor upon default under a mortgage, deed of trust, or security agreement.

(c) A transfer is made for present value if the exchange between the debtor and the transferee is intended by them to be contemporaneous and is in fact substantially contemporaneous.

§ 18–2–74: Transfer Made or Obligation Incurred by Debtor that is Fraudulent as to Creditor; Determination of Intent

(a) A transfer made or obligation incurred by a debtor is fraudulent as to a creditor, whether the creditor's claim arose before or after the transfer was made or the obligation was incurred, if the debtor made the transfer or incurred the obligation:

(1) With actual intent to hinder, delay, or defraud any creditor of the debtor; or

(2) Without receiving a reasonably equivalent value in exchange for the transfer or obligation, and the debtor:

> *(A) Was engaged or was about to engage in a business or a transaction for which the remaining assets of the debtor were unreasonably small in relation to the business or transaction; or*

> *(B) Intended to incur, or believed or reasonably should have believed that he or she would incur, debts beyond his or her ability to pay as they became due.*

(b) In determining actual intent under paragraph (1) of subsection (a) of this Code section, consideration may be given, among other factors, to whether:

> *(1) The transfer or obligation was to an insider;*

> *(2) The debtor retained possession or control of the property transferred after the transfer;*

> *(3) The transfer or obligation was disclosed or concealed;*

> *(4) Before the transfer was made or obligation was incurred, the debtor had been sued or threatened with suit;*

> *(5) The transfer was of substantially all the debtor's assets;*

> *(6) The debtor absconded;*

> *(7) The debtor removed or concealed assets;*

(8) *The value of the consideration received by the debtor was reasonably equivalent to the value of the asset transferred or the amount of the obligation incurred;*

(9) *The debtor was insolvent or became insolvent shortly after the transfer was made or the obligation was incurred;*

(10) *The transfer occurred shortly before or shortly after a substantial debt was incurred; and*

(11) *The debtor transferred the essential assets of the business to a lienor who transferred the assets to an insider of the debtor.*

§ 18–2–75: When Transfer Made or Obligation Incurred by Debtor is Fraudulent as to Creditor Whose Claim Arose Before Transfer Was Made

(a) A transfer made or obligation incurred by a debtor is fraudulent as to a creditor whose claim arose before the transfer was made or the obligation was incurred if the debtor made the transfer or incurred the obligation without receiving a reasonably equivalent value in exchange for the transfer or obligation and the debtor was insolvent at that time or the debtor became insolvent as a result of the transfer or obligation.

(b) A transfer made by a debtor is fraudulent as to a creditor whose claim arose before the transfer was made if the transfer was made to an insider for an antecedent debt, the debtor was insolvent at that time, and the insider had reasonable cause to believe that the debtor was insolvent.

§ 18–2–76: When Transfer is Made. *For the purposes of this article:*

(1) A transfer is made:

(A) With respect to an asset that is real property other than a fixture, but including the interest of a seller or purchaser under a contract for the sale of the asset, when the transfer is so far perfected that a good faith purchaser of the asset from the debtor against whom applicable law permits the transfer to be perfected cannot acquire an interest in the asset that is superior to the interest of the transferee; and

(B) With respect to an asset that is not real property or that is a fixture, when the transfer is so far perfected that a creditor on a simple contract cannot acquire a judicial lien otherwise than under this article that is superior to the interest of the transferee;

(2) If applicable law permits the transfer to be perfected as provided in paragraph (1) of this Code section and the transfer is not so perfected before the commencement of an action for relief under this article, the transfer is deemed made immediately before the commencement of the action;

(3) If applicable law does not permit the transfer to be perfected as provided in paragraph (1) of this Code section, the transfer is made when it becomes effective between the debtor and the transferee;

(4) A transfer is not made until the debtor has acquired rights in the asset transferred; and

(5) An obligation is incurred:

(A) If oral, when it becomes effective between the parties; or

(B) If evidenced by a writing, when the writing executed by the obligor is delivered to or for the benefit of the obligee.

§ 18–2–77: Relief for Creditor Against Fraudulent Transfer or Obligation

(a) In an action for relief against a transfer or obligation under this article, a creditor, subject to the limitations in Code Section 18–2–78, may obtain:

(1) Avoidance of the transfer or obligation to the extent necessary to satisfy the creditor's claim;

(2) An attachment or other provisional remedy against the asset transferred or other property of the transferee in accordance with the procedure prescribed by Chapter 3 of this title;

(3) Subject to applicable principles of equity and in accordance with applicable rules of civil procedure:

(A) An injunction against further disposition by the debtor or a transferee, or both, of the asset transferred or of other property;

(B) Appointment of a receiver to take charge of the asset transferred or of other property of the transferee; or

(C) Any other relief the circumstances may require.

(b) If a creditor has obtained a judgment on a claim against the debtor, the creditor, if the court so orders, may levy execution on the asset transferred or its proceeds.

§ 18–2–78: When Transfer or Obligation is Not Voidable

(a) A transfer or obligation is not voidable under paragraph (1) of subsection (a) of Code Section 18–2–74 against a person who took in good

faith and for a reasonably equivalent value or against any subsequent transferee or obligee.

(b) Except as otherwise provided in this Code section, to the extent a transfer is voidable in an action by a creditor under paragraph (1) of subsection (a) of Code Section 18–2–77, the creditor may recover judgment for the value of the asset transferred, as adjusted under subsection (c) of this Code section, or the amount necessary to satisfy the creditor's claim, whichever is less. The judgment may be entered against:

(1) The first transferee of the asset or the person for whose benefit the transfer was made; or

(2) Any subsequent transferee other than a good faith transferee or obligee who took for value or from any subsequent transferee or obligee.

(c) If the judgment under subsection (b) of this Code section is based upon the value of the asset transferred, the judgment must be for an amount equal to the value of the asset at the time of the transfer, subject to adjustment as the equities may require.

(d) Notwithstanding voidability of a transfer or an obligation under this article, a good faith transferee or obligee is entitled, to the extent of the value given the debtor for the transfer or obligation, to:

(1) A lien on or a right to retain any interest in the asset transferred;

(2) Enforcement of any obligation incurred; or

(3) A reduction in the amount of the liability on the judgment.

(e) A transfer is not voidable under paragraph (2) of subsection (a) of Code Section 18-2-74 or Code Section 18-2-75 if the transfer results from:

(1) Termination of a lease upon default by the debtor when the termination is pursuant to the lease and applicable law; or

(2) Enforcement of a security interest in compliance with Article 9 of the Uniform Commercial Code.

(f) A transfer is not voidable under subsection (b) of Code Section 18–2–75:

(1) To the extent the insider gave new value to or for the benefit of the debtor after the transfer was made unless the new value was secured by a valid lien;

(2) If made in the ordinary course of business or financial affairs of the debtor and the insider; or

(3) If made pursuant to a good faith effort to rehabilitate the debtor and the transfer secured the present value given for that purpose as well as an antecedent debt of the debtor.

§ 18-2-79: Statute of Limitations

A cause of action with respect to a fraudulent transfer or obligation under this article is extinguished unless action is brought:

(1) Under paragraph (1) of subsection (a) of Code Section 18–2–74, within four years after the transfer was made or the obligation was incurred or, if later, within one year after the transfer or obligation was or could reasonably have been discovered by the claimant;

(2) Under paragraph (2) of subsection (a) of Code Section 18–2–74 or subsection (a) of Code Section 18–2–75, within

four years after the transfer was made or the obligation was incurred; or

(3) Under subsection (b) of Code Section 18–2–75, within one year after the transfer was made or the obligation was incurred.

§ 18–2–80: Supplemental Laws; Transfers of Property in Determination of Eligibility for Public Benefits

(a) Unless displaced by the provisions of this article, the principles of law and equity, including the law merchant and the law relating to principal and agent, estoppel, laches, fraud, misrepresentation, duress, coercion, mistake, insolvency, or other validating or invalidating cause, supplement its provisions.

(b) The provisions of this article do not create a cause of action for a governmental entity or its agent or assignee with respect to a transaction which may otherwise constitute a fraudulent transfer or obligation under this article if the transaction complies with the applicable state and federal laws concerning transfers of property in the determination of eligibility for public benefits.

§ 18–2–81: Transfer to Charitable Organization

(a) As used in this Code section, the term:

(1) "Charitable organization" means an organization which has qualified as tax-exempt under Section 501(c)(3) of the federal Internal Revenue Code of 1986 and has been so qualified for not less than two years preceding any transfer pursuant to this Code section, other than a private foundation or family trust.

(2) "Private foundation" shall have the same meaning as set forth in 26 U.S.C. Section 509(a).

(b) A transfer made to a charitable organization shall be considered complete unless it is established that a fraudulent transfer has occurred as described in Code Section 18–2–74 or 18–2–75, and such charitable organization had knowledge of the fraudulent nature of the transfer.

(c) The statute of limitations for a civil action with respect to a transfer to a charitable organization under this Code section shall be within two years after such transfer was made.

A P P E N D I X   D

SAMPLE EMPLOYMENT AGREEMENT

Warning: As discussed at the beginning of this book these forms are intended as illustrations and are not intended for your use. You must consult your attorney about your particular situation and get legal advice on the proper contract for your situation.

EMPLOYMENT AGREEMENT

This employment agreement (this "Agreement") is made by and between _____, LLC, a Georgia limited liability company ("Employer"), and _____, an individual resident of Georgia (the "Employee"), effective as of the ___ day of _____, 2017 (the "Effective Date").

Whereas, the Employee wishes to become or to continue to be employed by Employer as _____ (describe position), and Employer wishes to employ or continue to employ Employee, and the parties hereto desire to set forth the terms and conditions under which Employee will serve or continue to serve in such capacity.

Now, therefore, for and in consideration of the foregoing, the mutual covenants contained herein, and other good and valuable consideration, the receipt and sufficiency of which are hereby acknowledged, the parties hereto, intending to be legally bound, hereby agree as follows:

Employer shall employ the Employee, and the Employee shall serve Employer, in the capacity of _____. The Employee shall be required to devote forty (40) hours each week to the performance of Employee's duties hereunder.

Employee's employment shall be "at will," meaning that Employee can terminate Employee's employment at any time for any reason and Employer can terminate Employee's employment at any time for any reason.

Employer shall pay Employee a salary at a rate of $_____ per annum [or $ _____ per hour] in accordance with the normal salary payment practices of Employer.

Employee shall be entitled to participate in all retirement, life and health insurance, disability and other similar benefit plans or programs of Employer now or hereafter applicable generally to employees of Employer. At present, Employer provides the following: _____.

Employer may withhold from any amounts of compensation payable under this Agreement all federal, state, city or other taxes and withholdings as shall be required pursuant to any applicable law, rule or regulation.

Employee consents to permit Employer to administer drug tests to detect for illegal drugs.

Employee consents to permit Employer to conduct background checks on Employee.

It is not the intent of any party hereto to violate any public policy of any jurisdiction in which this Agreement may be enforced. If any provision of this Agreement or the application of any provision hereof to any person or circum-stances is held invalid, unenforceable or otherwise illegal, the remainder of this Agreement and the application of such provision to any other person or circumstances shall not be affected, and the provision so held to be invalid, unenforceable or otherwise illegal shall be reformed to the extent (and only to the extent) necessary to make it valid, enforceable and legal.

This Agreement supersedes any other agreements, oral or written, between the parties with respect to the subject matter hereof, and contains all of the agreements and understandings between the parties with respect to the employment of Employee by Employer. Any waiver or modification of any term of this Agreement shall be effective only if it is set forth in a writing signed by all parties hereto.

No provisions of this Agreement may be modified, waived or discharged unless such waiver, modification or discharge is agreed to in writing and signed by the parties hereto. No waiver by any party hereto at any time of any breach by another party hereto of, or compliance with, any condition or provision of this Agreement to be performed by such other party shall be deemed a waiver of similar or dissimilar provisions or conditions at the same or at any prior or subsequent time.

This Agreement shall be governed by and construed and enforced in accordance with the laws of the State of Georgia without giving effect to the conflict of laws principles thereof.

MANDATORY ARBITRATION

Any controversy, claim or dispute arising from, out of or relating to this Agreement, or any breach thereof, including but not limited to any dispute concerning the scope of this arbitration clause, claims based in tort or contract, claims for discrimination under federal, state or local law, and/or claims for violation of any federal, state or local law ("Claims") shall be resolved in accordance with the National Rules for the Resolution of Employment Disputes of the American Arbitration Association then in effect. Such arbitration shall take place in Atlanta, Georgia. The arbitrator's award shall be final and binding upon both parties.

A demand for arbitration shall be made within a reasonable time after the Claim has arisen. In no event shall the demand for arbitration be made after the date when an institution of legal and/or equitable proceedings based on such Claim would be barred by the applicable statute of limitations. Each party to the arbitration will be entitled to be represented by counsel and shall have the right to subpoena witnesses and documents for the arbitration hearing. The arbitrator shall be experienced in employment arbitration and licensed to practice law in the state of Georgia. The arbitrator shall have the authority to hear and grant a motion to dismiss and/or motion for summary judgment, applying the standards governing such motions under the Federal Rules of Civil Procedure.

Each party shall pay the fees of its respective attorneys, the expenses of its witnesses and any other expenses connected with presenting its Claim or defense, but the party in whose favor the arbitrator rules shall be reimbursed for such party's attorney fee and expenses by the other party. Except as otherwise awarded by the arbitrator, other costs of arbitration, including arbitrator's fees and expenses, any transcript costs or other administrative fees shall be paid equally by the parties.

The parties indicate their acceptance of the foregoing arbitration requirement by initialing below:

_____   _____

Employer   Employee

IN WITNESS WHEREOF, the parties hereto have executed this Agreement, effective as of the Effective Date set forth herein.

_____, LLC: Employee:

By: _____   _____(SEAL)

Title: Managing Member

A P P E N D I X E

SAMPLE "PROLANDLORD" RESIDENTIAL REAL ESTATE LEASE

Warning: As discussed at the beginning of this book these forms are intended as illustrations and are not intended for your use. You must consult your attorney about your particular situation and get legal advice on the proper contract for your situation.

RESIDENTIAL LEASE AGREEMENT

1. LANDLORD AND TENANT: This Residential Lease Agreement (this "Lease" or "Agreement") is made and entered into on the ___ day of _____2017, by and between _____and ("Tenant") and ___ _____, LLC, a Georgia limited liability company ("Landlord"). If there is more than one (1) "Tenant," then each Tenant shall be jointly and severally liable and responsible for the payment of rent and the performance of all other terms and conditions of this Agreement.

2. THE PREMISES: Landlord rents to Tenant, and Tenant rents from Landlord, for residential the premises located at: _____ _____, _____(city), _____(county), Georgia, _____(zip code) ("the Premises"), together with the furnishings and appliances listed on the Inspection Form, as hereinafter defined.

3. LIMITS ON USE AND OCCUPANCY: The Premises are to be used only as a private residence for Tenant(s) listed in Section 1 of this Agreement, and the minor children of Tenant. Accordingly, only the following people are authorized to reside in and occupy the Premises:

a) _____ - adult

b) _____ - adult

c) _____ - child over 18 years of age

d) _____ - child under 18 years of age

e) _____ - child under 18 years of age

f) _____ - child under 18 years of age

The Premises shall not be used for any business purposes and no business activities shall be conducted at the Premises, including but not limited to a childcare facility/daycare of any kind. Occupancy by guests for more than twenty (20) days is prohibited without Landlord's prior written consent and will be considered a breach of this Agreement. The use and occupancy limits are subject to local laws.

The Premises shall be used by Tenant in strict compliance with all state, county, and municipal laws and ordinances, and any applicable community or homeowner association bylaws, rules and regulations. Tenant shall not use the Premises, or permit the Premises to be used, for any disorderly or unlawful purpose or in any manner so as to interfere with neighbors' quiet enjoyment of their dwellings.

Tenant shall not have any automobiles that are not in good working order at the Premises. Tenant agrees to abide by any and all protective covenants, by-laws or other regulations as set forth by the subdivision, condominium association or the community in which the Premises are located. Tenant further agrees that any violation of said covenants, by-laws, or regulations by Tenant will constitute a breach of this Agreement and Tenant will be responsible for any fine imposed by the association or community as a result of Tenant's violation. If the Premises is within a Home Owners Association, then the resident will be provided with a copy of the Covenants and Restrictions and Rules and Regulations upon request. Tenant has an obligation to adhere to the Home Owners Association rules and regulations. Any fines or violations assessed by the Home Owners Association will be charged back to the Tenant. Tenant shall conform to all restrictions of a Home Owners Association and shall cure any violation of the same immediately. Landlord reserves the right to correct any such violations at Tenant's sole expense.

4. TERM: The initial term of the lease shall be for a period beginning at 12 p.m. on the ___ day of _____, 2017 and ending at 11:59 am on the ____ day of _____, 2018; such period of time is known as the "Initial Term". Either party may terminate this Agreement at the end of the Initial Term by giving the other party at least sixty (60) days written notice prior to the end of the Initial Term. If no such notice is given by either party, then the Term of this Agreement will be automatically extended on a month-to-month basis at a rent equal to the rent stipulated in the lease renewal notice delivered by Landlord to Tenant, until terminated by either party thereafter, which termination shall require thirty (30) days prior written notice if terminated by Tenant or sixty (60) days prior written notice if terminated by Landlord. During such time as Tenant remains on a month-to-month basis, Landlord and Tenant shall remain bound by the terms of this Agreement; provided, however, that Landlord may alter the terms and conditions of this Agreement, including, without limitation, the amount of Rent due, upon sixty (60) days prior written notice to Tenant.

5. RENT: "Rent" shall mean all monetary obligations of Tenant. Base Rent is payable monthly in advance at a rate of $_____U.S. Dollars (per month) during the Term of this Agreement, on the first day of each calendar month, without notice or demand, at the office of Landlord or at such other place as Landlord may designate. Tenant bears sole responsibility for the timely delivery of Rent. Simply mailing the Rent does not constitute payment and will not absolve Tenant of its obligations hereunder. If the Term of this Lease commences after the 20th day of the month, then the initial base Rent payment due at Lease commencement will include the prorated rent amount for the initial month in addition to the full month's base Rent for the subsequent month. All funds referenced in this Agreement shall be in U.S. Dollars.

6. PAYMENTS: Time is of the essence of this Agreement. Tenant agrees that Landlord may apply payments at Landlord's sole discretion to any amount due from Tenant. Rent shall be paid using a cashier's check or money order, made payable to the Landlord, sent by U.S. mail, UPS or Federal Express to the following address: _____(street), _____ (city), Georgia _____ (zip code). Personal checks and cash are not acceptable forms of payment.

7. LATE PAYMENTS: Rent is due on the (1st) first day of each calendar month and is considered late if not received in Landlord's office by 5:00 p.m. (Eastern Time) on the fifth (5th) calendar day of the month. If Landlord agrees to accept payment after the fifth (5th) day of the month, Tenant must also pay Landlord the amount of [10% of rent] (_____) as a "Late Fee," plus interest on the outstanding amount due at a rate equal to the lesser of (i) eighteen percent (18%) per annum, or (ii) the maximum amount of interest allowable under applicable law. Tenant agrees to tender all Late Fees and interest amounts to Landlord in the form of cashier's check or money order. Landlord may, at its option, file dispossessory proceedings against Tenant if base Rent or any other amounts due under this Lease are not paid before 5:00 p.m. (Eastern Time) on the tenth (10th) calendar day of the month. In addition to all other amounts

Tenant is obligated to pay under this Agreement, Tenant also agrees to pay a $200.00 dispossessory administrative handling fee, court costs, and reasonable attorney fees if Landlord determines that a dispossessory action is necessary. The dispossessory fee shall be due at the time of filing Landlord's dispossessory action even if the summons is subsequently dismissed by Landlord or court action. Legal fees may be collected by the plaintiff or defendant in court if a judgment is reached in their respective favor.

In the case of a dispossessory action, upon obtaining a final judgment, legal fees and court costs (to the extent permissible under applicable law) may be collected by the winning party from the losing party. The parties are initialing below to evidence the foregoing understanding.

Tenant's Initials: _____

Landlord's Initials: _____

8. PARTIAL PAYMENTS: Tenant shall pay monthly account balances in full. Payment or receipt of a payment of less than the full amount shall be deemed to be nothing more than partial payment of that month's account balance. Under no circumstances shall Landlord's acceptance of a partial payment constitute accord or satisfaction of the total amount then due. Nor will Landlord's acceptance of a partial payment forfeit Landlord's right to collect the balance due on the account, despite any endorsement, stipulation, or other statement on Tenant's check. Landlord may accept any partial payment with any conditional endorsement without prejudice to the right to recover the balance remaining due, or to pursue any other remedy available. Any failure of Landlord to insist upon strict compliance with such payment terms and conditions shall not constitute a waiver of Landlords rights to thereafter insist upon or enforce any such term and or condition and such obligation shall remain in full force and effect. Landlord's acceptance of any partial payment of Rent or other monetary obligations does not waive Tenant's breach of any provision of the Lease nor any of Landlord's remedies as set forth herein.

9. RETURNED CHECKS: In the event a personal check or other form of payment is accepted for Rent, electronically or otherwise, Tenant hereby agrees to pay Landlord $40.00 or the maximum allowed by local laws as a handling charge and to reimburse Landlord for any damages suffered.

10. POSSESSION: Possession of the Premises to Tenant shall be granted at the beginning of the Initial Term. If there is a delay in delivery of possession by Landlord, payments shall be abated on a daily basis until possession is granted. Landlord shall not be liable for damages for delay in possession. In the event Tenant takes possession of the Premises during any day other than the first of the month, the monthly rent payment shall be prorated on the basis of a thirty-day period.

11. SECURITY DEPOSIT: Prior to Tenant tendering a security deposit, Landlord shall provide Tenant with Landlord's standard Move-In/Move-Out Inspection Form (the "Inspection Form"), as may be amended from time to time, for the purpose of identifying any existing damages to the Premises. A sample of an Inspection Form is attached as Exhibit A hereto and is incorporated herein by reference. Upon completion of the Inspection Form, the completed Inspection Form shall be attached to and deemed a part of this Agreement. Prior to taking actual occupancy, Tenant will be given the right to inspect the Premises to ascertain the accuracy of the Inspection Form. Both Landlord and Tenant shall sign the Inspection Form and Tenant shall be entitled to retain a copy of the Inspection Form. Tenant hereby acknowledges that Tenant has carefully inspected the Premises, is familiar with same and that the Premises are in a good and habitable condition. On signing this Agreement, and upon execution of the Inspection Form, Tenant will pay to Landlord the sum of $_____U.S. Dollars as security for Tenant's fulfillment of the conditions of this Agreement. The security deposit will be refunded to Tenant subject to the conditions set forth in this Agreement, without interest. Tenant may not apply the security deposit to the last month's Rent or to any other sum due under this Agreement. Landlord reserves the right to use the security deposit to satisfy any and all outstanding obligations of the Tenant under this Agreement. Subject to the terms and conditions of this Agreement, Landlord shall refund any unused portion of the security deposit (A) by the later of (i) within thirty (30) days after the end of the Term after the end of the Lease Term or (ii) Tenant has vacated and Landlord has taken possession of the Premises and (B) after deduction for (i) the satisfaction of all Rent, Late Fees and other payment amounts outstanding by Tenant and (iii) the payment of an amount equal to the estimated cost of any damage or repairs to the Premises during the Term, as determined by Landlord and reflected on an Inspection Form, other than normal wear and tear. Tenant shall have the right to inspect the Premises within five (5) business days after the termination of Tenant's occupancy in order to ascertain the accuracy of the estimated damages. Landlord and Tenant shall sign the list, and Tenant shall express in writing the items on the Inspection Form to which Tenant dissents and shall sign such statement of dissent. In the event Tenant fails to inspect the Premises or sign the Inspection Form reflecting estimated damages, Tenant hereby waives any and all objections thereto and is deemed to have acknowledged and agreed to such estimated damages.

Landlord shall be deemed to have complied with Georgia law by mailing the statement and any payment required to the last known address of Tenant. If the letter containing the security deposit refund payment is returned to Landlord undelivered, and if Landlord is unable to locate Tenant after exercising commercially reasonable efforts, the security deposit payment amount shall become the property of Landlord ninety (90) days after the date the payment was mailed. Everything concerning the security deposit refund shall be recorded in writing.

If Tenant defaults on this Lease, the security deposit, in its entirety, will be forfeited to Landlord. The parties are initialing below to evidence the foregoing understanding.

Tenant's Initials: _____

Landlord's Initials: _____

12. APPLICATION: Tenant has completed and signed an application to lease the Premises. Landlord is entering into this Lease with Tenant based on the accuracy and completeness of the information supplied by Tenant in the application. If any of the information in the application is not accurate and complete, then Tenant shall be in breach of this Agreement and Landlord shall have the right to terminate this Lease. If any information in the application changes (such as Tenant's employment), then Tenant agrees to inform Landlord immediately in writing of the changed information.

13. PETS: No animals, birds, insects, reptiles, or other pets (hereinafter called Pets) of any kind shall be permitted (even temporarily) without Landlord's written consent. Landlord reserves the right to revoke Landlord's consent on three (3) days' prior notice to Tenant, if in the sole judgment of Landlord the pet (i) has been a nuisance to Tenants, neighbors or surrounding community, or (ii) has damaged the Premises. If Tenant is permitted to have a pet or pets within the Premises, Tenant agrees to pay a $250.00 fee for the first pet and, if applicable, a $250.00 for each additional pet for which Landlord's written consent has been obtained. Pet fees are non-refundable and shall be paid by Tenant to Landlord before the pet is permitted to at the Premises. Further, Tenant shall cause all carpets in the Premises to be commercially cleaned and deodorized at least annually and, upon termination of this Agreement, to pay for all damage to the Premises (doors, hardwood floors, carpets, etc.) caused either wholly or in part by the pet(s). In no case are the following breeds (or any other breeds which would cause Landlord's insurance to increase or otherwise be adversely affected), whether full or partial, allowed: Chows, Rottweilers, Dobermans, German Shepherds, American Terriers (Pit Bulls), and Saint Bernards. Landlord reserves the right to amend or update this list of restricted breeds from time to time, in Landlord's sole discretion.

14. SMOKING: Smoking is expressly prohibited within the confines of the Premises without written consent of Landlord. If smoking is allowed by Landlord, Tenant agrees to pay a $500.00 fee to Landlord before any smoking is permitted on or within the Premises. Tenant acknowledges that smoking within the Premises can and will cause a need for additional Tenant responsibilities including, but not limited to, additional cleaning, deodorizing and painting of the Premises. Tenant accepts the responsibility for the costs of these additional maintenance needs. Landlord suggests that if Tenant must smoke that Tenant smoke outside and within a suitable distance from the Premises. Tenant will be required to pay Landlord $300.00 per month for each unauthorized smoker found on the Premises during the Term of this Lease. The foregoing payment by Tenant   shall be made in arrears from the date the unauthorized smoker(s) first appeared on the Premises, as determined solely by Landlord, and if Tenant vacates the Premises and the Premises contains smoke-related odors, as determined solely by Landlord, Tenant shall promptly pay Landlord a $5500.00 administrative fee in connection with such event, unless and except to the extent Tenant has previously paid Landlord in full for all the amounts due under this Section 14.

15. SIGNS: Tenant shall not display any signs, exterior lights or marking on the Premises. No awnings or other projections shall be attached to the outside of any building or structure constituting or relating to the Premises. Landlord may place signage in the yard sixty (60) days or less prior to the end of the Term. In addition, Landlord may install a lock box and show the Premises to prospective lessees or purchasers during the last sixty (60) days of the Term, or at such time as Landlord may choose to sell the Premises.

16. PARKING: Off-street parking is provided in designated areas. No on-street parking or parking on the lawn of Premises is allowed. Non-operative vehicles are not permitted on the Premises. Landlord, at the expense of Tenant, may remove any non-operative vehicle for storage or public or private sale, at Landlord's option, and Tenant owning same shall have no right of recourse against Landlord. Tenant is responsible for oil leaks and other vehicular discharges for which Tenant shall be charged for cleaning if deemed necessary by Landlord. If inoperable vehicles are not removed or repaired as requested the Landlord has the right to tow the vehicle within 48 hours at Tenants expense.

17. STORAGE: No goods or materials of any kind or description, which are combustible or would increase fire risk shall be placed at the Premises.

18. WALLS: No nails, screws, or adhesive hangers except standard picture hooks, shade brackets and curtain rod brackets may be placed in walls, woodworks or any part of the building.

19. BALCONIES & PATIOS: Balcony or patio shall be kept neat and clean at all times. No rugs, towels, laundry, clothing or other items shall be stored, hung or draped on railings or other portions of the balcony or patio. Gas or charcoal gilling on balconies or patios is prohibited.

20. UTILITIES; PHONE, CABLE & INTERNET SERVICES: Tenant shall establish prior to possession, and maintain during the term of this Agreement, all utility accounts for the Premises. Unless otherwise agreed in writing, payment to the utility company of the applicable deposits, fees, and charges for gas, electricity or water consumed by Tenant in the Premises and to connect and disconnect service to the Premises shall be the sole responsibility of Tenant. Tenant shall also be solely responsible for cable and telephone service. Upon termination of this Lease, Tenant will coordinate with Landlord to ensure the orderly transfer of utilities such that no interruptions occur in utility services. Tenant agrees to pay Landlord an administrative handling fee of $25.00 per payment for any utility payments made by Landlord for the Premises during the Term of this Lease, together with full reimbursement to Landlord of any amounts Landlord has so paid with respect to utility services. Such costs shall be immediately due and payable upon notice by Landlord. Failure of Tenant to establish any utilities in Tenant's name shall be deemed a default by Tenant hereunder. If utilities are disconnected as a result of nonpayment by Tenant, the Tenant will be in default of the lease. Tenant shall be responsible for any utility charges from the commencement date of this Lease. Such costs will be due immediately and payable by Tenant upon notice by Landlord. Prior to termination of this Agreement, Tenant will coordinate with Landlord to ensure the orderly transfer of utilities such that no interruptions in utility services exist. Any further fines, violations, or illegal use deemed by a utility company will be charged to Tenant.

Availability of telephone service, Internet service, satellite or cable television service or any other service to the Premises is not guaranteed, and any installation or repair charges are the sole responsibility of Tenant. Installation of any such service at the Premises shall occur only with the written approval of Landlord and any damages to the Premises as a result of such installation including, but not limited to, holes in the walls or floors, shall be the responsibility of the Tenant and shall not be considered normal wear and tear. Tenant agrees to coordinate the visit/installation/service of all said service providers with Landlord. Radio or television aerials shall not be placed or erected on the roof or exterior of buildings. Pole mounts independent of any building are allowed.

21. SUBLETTING; ASSIGNMENT: Tenant may not sublet all or any portion of the Premises, or assign or transfer this Lease without the prior written consent of Landlord, which consent can be withheld in Landlord's sole discretion. Unless such consent is validly obtained, any assignment, transfer or subletting of the Premises or this Lease or tenancy, by voluntary act of Tenant, operation of law or otherwise, will, at the option of Landlord, terminate this Lease. Landlord's consent to any one assignment, transfer or sublease will not be construed as consent to any subsequent, assignment, transfer or sublease and does not release Tenant of Tenant's obligations under this Lease. Landlord may assign this Agreement in its sole and absolute discretion without notice.

22. WATERBEDS: Waterbeds are prohibited.

23. DISCLOSURE: Tenant hereby acknowledges, prior to tendering any security deposit, that Tenant is in receipt of the Inspection Form identifying any existing damages to the Premises known to Landlord, Tenant has inspected the Premises, accepts the Premises in its "as is" condition and hereby confirms the Premises as being suitable for the Residential Tenant use intended by Tenant.

24. INSPECTIONS/SURVEYS (QUARTERLY): Landlord has the right, at its sole option, to perform quarterly inspections/surveys to perform property condition assessments. Tenant agrees to coordinate with Landlord for the timely performance of such inspections/surveys. Tenant agrees to allow Landlord to make audio and video recordings of the Premises even if such activity includes the recording of Tenant's personal property and of persons occupying the Premises. Any recording of Tenant's property and such persons are incidental to the record of the Premises' condition.

25. KEROSENE HEATERS: The use of kerosene or fuel oil heaters in or about the Premises is expressly and strictly prohibited.

26. LANDSCAPE/OUTSIDE CARE: Tenant agrees to provide regular and routine landscape care including, but not limited to, edging, irrigation, weed control, shrub and tree trimming, lawn mowing, removal of sticks and fallen branches, pine island and mulch rejuvenation, snow and ice removal, gutter cleaning, lawn overseeding, and leaf removal. Tenant agrees to properly dispose of landscape debris (not to be stored or composted on the Premises). Tenant agrees entrances, driveways, walks, lawns and other public areas shall not be obstructed or used for any purpose other than ingress and egress. If Landlord observes Tenant to be deficient in any of these activities on a regular or routine basis, Landlord reserves the right to either perform the service, or to hire the appropriate contractor to perform such services, in either instance at Tenant's cost, which shall be considered an additional Rent. The minimum service call charge for Landlord's lawn maintenance services is $75 per service call.

27. PEST CONTROL: Once Tenant takes possession, Tenant agrees to provide, at Tenant's expense, pest control and extermination services (other than termite control, which shall remain Landlord's responsibility) as needed on the Premises and agrees to maintain the Premises in a clean and sanitary condition in order to avoid problems with insect infestation. Reference to "pests" shall be deemed to include, but not be limited to, ants, fleas, mice, rats and other types of garden and household pests. Tenant shall notify Landlord immediately of any suspected evidence of termites. In addition, Tenant agrees to obtain a pest control service (which includes rodent control) for the Premises from a firm doing commercial business in the general area of the Premises, and to provide Landlord with proof of the pest control service at move in and promptly upon Landlord's request.

28. ALTERATION: Tenant may not remodel, alter, paint or structurally change the Premises, nor remove any fixtures therein without Landlord's prior written consent. In the event of any alterations, painting, or structural changes to the Premises without Landlord's prior written consent, Tenant will be billed the costs to return the Premises to its original condition. Any alterations or changes which Landlord does permit shall become the property of Landlord, and shall remain in or on the Premises at all times during and after the Term hereof. Tenant has no authority to incur debt or make any charge against the Premises or Landlord, or to create any lien upon said Premises for work done or materials furnished, or to act as agent for Landlord at any time or for any purpose.

29. MAINTENANCE: Tenant shall maintain the Premises in as good a condition as on the date of possession, ordinary wear and tear excepted, and shall keep the Premises, including the yard, in clean and orderly condition. Tenant has examined the Premises, including appliances, fixtures, carpets, drapes and paints, and has found them to be in good, safe and clean condition and repair, except as noted in the Move-In Inspection Form.

30. LOCKS/RE-KEYING: Tenant may not alter or install locks without Landlord's written consent and all keys shall be returned upon Tenant vacating the Premises. Tenant acknowledges that new locks have been installed at the Premises after being vacated by the previous tenant. Tenant understands the opportunity to have the Premises re-keyed at a cost of $125.00. In the event Landlord agrees to any additional locks, Tenant agrees to provide Landlord a key or operating device thereto at Tenant's expense. Any such additional lock shall remain affixed to the Premises upon termination of this Agreement and shall become the property of Landlord at the time of installation. Upon termination of this Agreement, Tenant shall pay Landlord the amount of $250.00 for the cost of (i) re-keying or replacing any locks for which all keys are not returned, and (ii) replacing locks that Tenant has changed. Landlord does not provide mail box keys for town home residences. Tenant shall be responsible for the cost of re-keying mail box locks. At the end of this Lease, Landlord will reimburse Tenant $25.00 if all keys are returned to Landlord.

31. REPAIRS: Tenant acknowledges that Tenant has inspected the Premises, accepts the Premises in an as-is condition and agrees to maintain and return the Premises in the same condition, except for normal wear and tear. Landlord agrees to make repairs to the Premises that are reasonably necessary or required by law, including the structural, electrical, heating, air conditioning (if applicable), plumbing and hot water with reasonable promptness after receipt of written notice from Tenant. Tenant agrees to immediately notify Landlord of any repair or circumstance or condition which might cause damage to the Premises or which might threaten the health or safety of any person. Failure to promptly notify Landlord of any defective condition shall relieve Landlord of all liability for damages or obligations of any nature arising out of or relating to such defective condition. Repairs may be completed by an independent contractor and not an employee or agent of the Landlord. Notifying the independent contractor of a subsequent problem/repair is not notifying Landlord and failure to do so may lead to tenant being responsible for all or a portion of any damages.

Please contact Landlord at – (telephone number) between the hours of 9:00 a.m. to 5:30 p.m. (Eastern Time) Monday through Friday. Emergency repair requests should be made to Landlord via telephone, together with written notification within 24 hours of such telephonic notice.

32. RIGHT OF ACCESS: Landlord (including independent contractors or employees of maintenance and repair services employed or hired by Landlord) shall have the right of access the Premises during reasonable hours, without notice, for purposes of inspecting and maintaining the Premises for any purpose, or to show the Premises to perspective lessees or buyers. In case of an emergency, Landlord may enter the Premises at any time to protect life or to prevent or minimize damage to the Premises. Tenant may not change any locks on the Premises or add additional locking devices to the Premises without Landlord's prior written consent. Tenant authorizes Landlord to install a lockable key box to show the Premises during reasonable hours to prospective lessees or purchasers and, further, Tenant specifically agrees to cooperate with Landlord and/or Landlord's management company (or other agents of Landlord) (i) after Tenant has given notice of Lease termination, (ii) within sixty (60) days of Lease expiration, or (iii) during any period when the Premises are being leased on a month-to-month basis. For each occasion where the access rights described above are denied, Tenant agrees to pay Landlord the sum of $250.00 as liquidated damages; it being acknowledged that Landlord shall be damaged by the denial of access, that Landlord's actual damages are hard to estimate, and that the above amount represents a reasonable estimate of Landlord's damages and does not constitute, nor do the parties deem that it will constitute, a penalty.

33. DAMAGES: Tenant shall be responsible for any and all repairs or damage beyond normal wear and tear, including but not limited to items listed on Exhibit B attached hereto and incorporate herein ("Tenant Repairs Reference List"). If any damage to the Premises is caused or permitted to be caused by Tenant, Tenant's guests or invites, Landlord may, at Landlord's sole option, repair or pay for the repair of such damage, and Tenant shall immediately reimburse Landlord for the total cost of such repairs and for the replacement cost of all property so destroyed or damaged. Such costs shall be immediately due and payable when incurred by Landlord. Tenant shall be responsible for any damage to plumbing, cooling or heating apparatus and other equipment, including but not limited to stove, refrigerator, dishwasher and disposal resulting from misuse or negligence by Tenant. Tenant shall not use water closets, drains or other plumbing apparatus for any other purpose than those for which they were constructed, and shall not throw sweepings, rubbish, rags, ashes or other substances therein.

34. PROPERTY LOSS: If the Premises are rendered unfit for occupancy by fire or other casualty not the fault of Tenant, or by storm, earthquake or other natural disaster, this Lease shall terminate as of the date of such destruction or damage and Rent shall be accounted for as of that date. Tenant releases, holds harmless, and indemnifies Landlord from and against any and all claims for loss or casualty.

35. CONDEMNATION: If any portion of the Premises is taken by any public authority by eminent domain, this Lease shall terminate effective as of the date of such taking and Tenant shall not, on and after such date, be obligated to pay Rent or any other charges with respect to the Premises to the extent such amounts have not yet accrued. Tenant hereby assigns to Landlord all condemnation awards of any nature arising out of or relating to Tenant's interest created by this Lease.

36. PERSONAL PROPERTY; TENANT'S INSURANCE: Tenant shall maintain insurance for Tenant's personal property in an amount satisfactory to Tenant. Landlord shall not maintain insurance to protect Tenant's personal property, and shall not be liable for any damage to Tenant's property. Tenant represents and warrants to Landlord that all personal property placed or stored by Tenant in the Premises shall be Tenant's own property and shall be subject to levy and sale under distress warrant or other legal process. Tenant, on behalf of Tenant and Tenant's family, hereby waives all exemptions or benefits under the homestead laws of Georgia. Landlord shall also have the right to store or dispose of any of Tenant's property remaining on the Premises after the termination of this Agreement or the abandonment of the Premises by Tenant. Any such property shall be considered Landlord's property and title thereto shall vest in Landlord without further action or agreement by Tenant. Renters insurance is required and a copy of the declarations page must be provided to the Landlord at move in. The renter's insurance policy must be maintained for the term of the lease or it shall constitute a default under the lease.

37. TERMINATION: Landlord or Tenant may terminate this Agreement without cause at the end of the initial Term by delivering to the other party sixty (60) days written notice prior to the end of the initial Term. If no such notice of termination is delivered, then this Agreement shall be deemed automatically renewed on a month-to-month basis. This Lease may be subject to immediate termination for certain acts as provided by local laws, including any act that jeopardizes the health, safety or welfare of Landlord, any agent or employee of Landlord, or another Resident, or which involves imminent or actual severe personal injury or property damage.

38. EARLY TERMINATION: Provided Tenant is not in default hereunder at the time of giving the notice, strictly complies with all the provisions of this Section 38, and termination is as of the last day of a calendar month, Tenant may terminate this Agreement before the expiration of the initial Term by: (a) giving Landlord sixty (60) days' prior written notice on or before the day Tenant's Rent payment is due, (b) paying all other sums due through date of termination, (c) paying an amount equal to one month's base Rent as liquidated damages, and (d) paying a prorated portion of the amount of $1,200.00 for the expenses associated with advertising, cleaning, painting and utility changes. The prorating shall be based on the ratio of the number of months remaining in the initial Term of the Lease to the total number of months in the initial Term. In addition to the foregoing payments, to effectuate such early termination Tenant hereby agrees to have all the carpets in the Premises professionally cleaned, and to provide Landlord with a copy of the receipt evidencing that such cleaning has been completed and fully paid for. The foregoing shall not relieve the Tenant of Tenant's responsibilities and obligations regarding any damages to the Premises or the Landlord's right to apply the security deposit to the same. During or after the Term of this Lease, Tenant authorizes Landlord to report any unsatisfied obligations to the proper authorities and to recover any amounts Tenant owes in connection therewith. Landlord may terminate this Lease prior to the lease expiration date and, in such event, Tenant agrees to vacate the Premises subject to the following: (y) Landlord shall give Tenant prior written notice of the early termination and to vacate (in which case Tenant shall still owe rent through the notice period), and (z) after Tenant has vacated the Premises, Landlord shall credit to Tenant the Early Termination Fee of one month's Rent as liquidated damages for disturbing Tenant's quiet enjoyment of the Premises and for the inconvenience of moving early. This credit shall be applied to the Tenant account at the time Tenant vacates the Premises and shall be deducted against any Rent, Late Fees or other payments or estimated damages. The foregoing shall not relieve Tenant of his or her responsibilities and obligations regarding any damage to the Premises.

39. RENT AFTER INITIAL TERM; PER DIEM CHARGES: The monthly base Rent payable by Tenant will automatically increase by $100/month if this Agreement is extended on a month to month basis. In addition, Landlord reserves the right to further increase the amount of base Rent subsequent to the initial Term upon delivery of written notice to Tenant thirty (30) days prior to the effective date of any increase. Tenant will be billed $50.00 per day for not providing Landlord possession of the Premises under the terms of this Agreement.

40. SURRENDER: Whenever Landlord is entitled to possession of the Premises under the terms of this Lease, Tenant shall at once surrender the Premises to Landlord and shall remove all of Tenant's property. Should Tenant remain after termination or expiration of this Lease, Tenant shall be deemed a Tenant at sufferance.

41. ABANDONMENT; STORAGE OF PROPERTY: If Tenant and all authorized occupants appear to have moved out of the Premises during the Term, while all or any portion of the Rent is delinquent, the Premises and any property of Tenant shall be deemed abandoned. In the event of such abandonment, Landlord shall have the right, without notice, to store or dispose of any property left on the Premises by Tenant. Further, Landlord shall have the right to store or dispose of any of Tenant's property remaining on the Premises after the termination or expiration of this Agreement. Any such property shall be considered Landlord's property and title thereto shall vest in Landlord with the necessity of consent or further action by Tenant. Landlord shall take action subject to local laws.

42. DEFAULT: In the event of a non-monetary default, upon written notice Tenant will have five (5) days to cure the default. In the event of a failure to pay a monetary charge when due, then upon written notice, Tenant will have three (3) days to cure the monetary default. Upon the failure to cure a default, Landlord may (a) continue the Lease in effect and enforce all rights and remedies under the Lease, including the right to recover the Rent as it comes due, (b) terminate Tenant's rights and recover all damages caused by Tenant's breach of the Lease, and/or (c) assert all legal and contractual remedies to enforce this Lease without terminating the Lease including, without limitation to any other remedy, sue for a dispossessory warrant and have Tenant and Tenant's family evicted from the Premises and Tenant's property removed. The selection of one remedy may not preclude the election of another remedy. The Tenant will only be allowed to cure a default once during the Term.

43. CARPET CLEANING OBLIGATION: Tenant is required upon termination of this Lease to have all carpets professionally cleaned by one of the following approved companies: (1) Fiber Care, (2) Stanley Steamer, or (3) Sears or such other vendor as Landlord may direct. If carpets are not professionally cleaned and a receipt is not provided, $350.00 will be charged to Tenant.

44. REPORTING AUTHORIZATION: During or after the term of this Agreement, Tenant authorizes Landlord to report any unsatisfied obligations to the proper authorities.

45. INDEMNIFICATION: Tenant releases Landlord from liability for and agrees to indemnify Landlord against all losses incurred by Landlord as a result of (i) Tenant's failure to fulfill any condition of this Agreement, (ii) any damage or injury happening in or about the Premises to Tenant's invitees or guests or any such person's property, (iii) Tenant's failure to comply with any requirements imposed by any governmental authority, or (d) any judgment, lien or other encumbrance filed against the Premises as a result of Tenant's actions.

46. ATTORNEY'S FEES AND COSTS OF COLLECTION: In any legal action to enforce the terms hereof or relating to the Premises, the prevailing party shall be entitled to all costs incurred in connection with such action, including reasonable attorney's fees, plus all costs of collection.

47. NOTICES: Any notice required by this agreement shall be in writing and shall be deemed to be given immediately if delivered personally or refused, and upon receipt or three (3) days after mailing by registered or certified mail, return receipt requested, or by standard overnight delivery as provided by O.C.G.A. § 9-10-12(b): (a) if to Tenant, to the Premises or the last known address of Tenant; (b) if to Landlord, to the address listed in Section 6 of this Lease. Tenant hereby appoints any other adult authorized to occupy the Premises at the time as Tenant's agent to receive the service of any dispossessory or similar proceedings and all notices required or delivered under this Lease, and if no such other adult is in occupancy of the Premises, then such service or notice may be made by attaching the same on the front entrance of the Premises.

48. NO WAIVER; REMEDIES CUMULATIVE: Any failure of Landlord to seek redress for the violation of, or to insist upon the strict and prompt performance of, any covenants or conditions of this Lease or any of the rules and regulations determined by Landlord, shall not operate as a waiver of any such violation or of Landlord's right to insist on prompt compliance in the future of such covenant or condition, and shall not prevent a subsequent action by Landlord for any such violation. The receipt of any Rent or other amount by Landlord with the knowledge of a breach shall not operate as a waiver of such breach. No provision, covenant or condition of this Lease may be waived by Landlord unless such waiver is in writing and signed by Landlord. All remedies under this Agreement or by law or equity shall be cumulative.

49. MORTGAGEE'S RIGHTS: Tenant's rights under this Lease shall at all times be automatically junior and subject to any mortgage, deed of trust, or deed to secure debt which is now or shall hereafter be placed on the Premises or any part thereof. If requested by Landlord, Tenant shall execute promptly any certificate that Landlord may request to specifically implement the subordination of Tenant's rights as set forth in this Section 51.

50. ADDITIONAL RULES AND REGULATIONS: Landlord reserves the right to establish additional rules, make changes to the lease, and regulations, as he deems appropriate upon thirty (30) days written notice to Tenant.

51. MOLD: Landlord is not aware of any chronic water intrusion, flooding or other condition existing on the Premises as of the date of this Lease that would contribute to the proliferation of mold and mildew so as to cause mold contamination of the Premises. Tenant hereby acknowledges and agrees that, as of the date of this Lease, the Premises are habitable, and no mold contamination exists on the Premises. During the Term, Tenant agrees and is obligated to provide Landlord with prompt written notice of the suspected presence of mold and mildew, chronic water intrusion or flooding on the Premises or any part thereof. Tenant shall, following any such notice, make the Premises available to the Landlord for assessment and, if necessary, remediation. Tenant agrees to take action to prevent mold from forming by cleaning areas where moisture is located. In the event Landlord determines that remediation is necessary, Landlord shall be entitled to terminate this Lease upon twenty (20) days written notice to Tenant without premium or penalty. Landlord is not responsible for damages or losses due to mold growth to the extent resulting from Tenant failing to comply with measures to prevent mold or mildew.

52. LEAD-BASED PAINT DISCLOSURE: Housing built before 1978 may contain lead-based paint. Lead from paint, paint chips, and dust can pose health hazards if not taken care of properly. Before renting pre-1978 housing, lessors must disclose the presence of known lead-based paint and/or lead-based paint hazards in the dwelling. If applicable, Tenant acknowledges receipt of the EPA's "Protect Your Family from Lead in Your Home" pamphlet.

53. APPLIANCES: The appliances identified in on the Move-In Inspection Form are delivered with the Premises and are for the use and convenience of Tenant. Tenant acknowledges that these appliances are in good condition and working order at the beginning of the Term but are not guaranteed to operate for the duration of this Agreement. Tenant shall be responsible for normal and routine maintenance on all appliances and shall return same clean and in similar working condition at the end of this Lease. Tenant shall not remove or discard appliances. If Tenant removes any appliances, it is considered theft and it will be reported to the local authorities.

54. CARBON MONOXIDE DETECTORS: Tenant is responsible for obtaining and maintaining carbon monoxide detectors, including battery replacement.

55. FIRE DETECTION EQUIPMENT: Tenant acknowledges the placement and proper operation of all required fire protection equipment and agrees to maintain same in proper working order including the periodic testing thereof and the replacement of batteries. Tenant agrees to notify Landlord immedi-ately in writing if any fire detection equipment is found to be inoperative.

56. FIREPLACE USE: If a fireplace is in the Premises, and such fireplace is equipped with gas logs, natural gas is the only combustible material to be used in the fireplace. If the fireplace is not equipped with gas logs, Tenant agrees to burn only seasoned hardwoods in the fireplace.

57. FROZEN OR BROKEN WATER PIPES: During cold weather, Tenant agrees to maintain sufficient heat necessary to avoid pipes from freezing on the Premises. When the temperature is to be below 20 degrees Fahrenheit, the faucets inside the house and the outside hose faucet are to be left on with a small drip (not steady stream) to prevent frozen or broken water pipes. The exterior faucets are to be wrapped with some form of insulation and such insulation must be secured with suitable duct tape or fastening string so that the insulation will not blow off. Damage to plumbing, the Premises, and/or personal property from frozen or broken water pipes will not be considered normal wear and tear and will be charged to Tenant.

58. SCREENS: There may or may not be screens for each and every window/door. Existing screens may be installed in existing openings if Tenant so desires, but at Tenant's sole cost and expense. Landlord does not and will not procure or maintain the screens. If the Premises do not have screens at the time of the Lease signing, screens will not be provided by Landlord nor replaced.

59. GUESTS AND INVITEES: Tenant shall be responsible and liable for the conduct of Tenant's guests and invitees. Acts of guests and invitees in violation of this Agreement or Landlord's rules and regulations may, at Landlord's option, be deemed an event of default under this Agreement. At no time will Tenant permit any guests, visitors or other persons to reside at the Premises for any extended period of time (i.e., more than 20 days, in the aggregate, whether consecutively or otherwise, during the Term of this Agreement) without first having obtained the prior written consent of Landlord. Tenant will be required to pay Landlord $200.00 per month, in arrears, for each unauthorized guest, visitor or other person violating this Section 61 from the date the violation first occurred until cured, as determined solely by Landlord.

60. TOILETS/CLOGGED TOILETS: Tenant has confirmed that all toilets are in proper working order. Tenant is responsible for maintaining toilets in good working condition at Tenant's sole expense, including but not limited to repairs related to clogs, running water and similar conditions. Tenant should call a licensed plumber for all toilet and related repairs. Landlord is not responsible for unclogging toilets.

61. ADDITIONAL RENT: In addition to the payment of rent, Tenant also covenants and agrees to pay to Landlord all expenses which Landlord may suffer or incur by reason of any default of the provisions of this Lease, including, without limitation, the costs incurred in re-letting the Premises, as well as the cost of repairing damage to the Premises caused by the acts of the Tenant, or by any of Tenant's family, guests, invitees or other persons visiting with Tenant or Tenant's family. All charges under this Section 62 shall be deemed to consti-tute additional Rent due and payable upon Landlord's notice to Tenant of the occurrence thereof.

62. RESTRICTED GARBAGE SERVICE: Certain municipalities and areas restrict garbage service from being set up under Tenant's name, and instead require that it is turned on and kept under Landlord's name. If after signing this Lease the garbage company advises that garbage service is required to be set up under Landlord's name, Tenant will be required to reimburse Landlord for such expense.

63. NEIGHBORHOOD CONDITIONS: Tenant acknowledges that in every neighborhood there are conditions which different tenants may find objectionable. It shall be Tenant's duty to become acquainted with any present or future neighborhood conditions which could affect the Premises including, without limitation, land-fills, quarries, high-voltage power lines, cemeteries, airports, stadiums, odor producing factories, crime, schools serving the Premises, political jurisdictional maps and land use and transportation maps and plans. If Tenant is concerned about the possibility of a registered sex offender residing in the neighborhood in which Tenant is interested, Tenant should review the Georgia Violent Sex Offender Registry available on the Georgia Bureau of Investigation website at www.state.ga.us/gbi/disclaim.html.

Tenant understands that it is Tenant's duty to become acquainted with any present or future neighborhood conditions, which could affect the Premises or Tenant's property including, without limitation, each of the conditions listed in this Section. The parties are initialing below to evidence the foregoing understanding.

Tenant's Initials: _____

Landlord's Initials: _____

64. PROPERTY REPRESENTATION: Tenant agrees that Landlord has properly and accurately represented the Premises to Tenant, including all the features, appliances, furnishings, and amenities. Tenant has conducted its own due diligence concerning the Premises, and Tenant's decision to enter into this Lease was not based or dependent upon any descriptions or representations by Landlord or any agent or representative of Landlord. I (the Tenant) have not relied on management's description of this property.

65. ENTIRE AGREEMENT: This Lease and any attached exhibits and addenda constitute the entire agreement and understanding between the parties, and no representation, inducement, warranty, promise, agreement, oral or otherwise not expressly set forth herein shall be binding upon the parties hereto or have any legal force and effect whatsoever.

66. NOTICES: The address to send Notices for Tenant shall be the Premises. The address to send notices for Landlord is as follows: _____
_____, Georgia _____.

IN WITNESS WHEREOF, the parties hereto have set their hand and seal as of the day and year first above written.

TENANT(s) (Jointly & Severally):

_____(SEAL) (signature)

_____(print name)

_____(SEAL) (signature)

_____(print name)

_____ (SEAL) (signature)

_____(print name)

LANDLORD:

_____, LLC, a Georgia limited liability company

By: _____, Authorized Representative

© Copyright 2014 Harold Hudson

Printed in the USA
CPSIA information can be obtained
at www.ICGtesting.com
JSHW012031140824
68134JS00033B/2987

9 781599 325293